THE COOK'S GUIDE TO MEAT

THE COOK'S GUIDE TO MEAT

Jennie Milsom

Illustrated by Jane Laurie

APPLE

A Quintet Book

First published in the UK in 2009 by
Apple Press
7 Greenland Street
London NW1 0ND
United Kingdom

www.apple-press.com

ISBN: 978-1-84543-332-1
QTT.GGM

This book was conceived, designed and produced by
Quintet Publishing Limited
The Old Brewery, 6 Blundell Street
London N7 9BH, UK

Project Editor: Robert Davies
Designer: Emma Wicks
Copy Editor: Nicole Foster
Art Director: Michael Charles
Managing Editor: Donna Gregory
Publisher: James Tavendale

10 9 8 7 6 5 4 3 2 1

Printed in China by 1010 Printing International Limited

CONTENTS

What is meat?

Today, we often take for granted how easy and convenient it is to buy meat. For most of us it is hard to imagine having to trek further than our local butcher or supermarket to choose from a wide selection of meat that has been carefully processed, preserved and packaged. Yet everyday life for our ancestors was very different. Their diet, like ours, consisted of a mixture of meat and vegetables but the way they went about finding it was a much more hands-on experience. Animals and fish were hunted and killed with spears; berries, nuts, insects and vegetables were foraged from bushes and trees. Venturing out into the wild with handmade tools to slaughter an animal and drag the bloody carcass home was as normal for our ancestors as jumping in a car and heading to the supermarket is for us.

Over the years, the word 'meat' has come to mean the flesh of animals prepared for eating. It consists of water, protein and fat and is made up of bundles of long, thin muscle fibres which become the recognizable grain of the meat. These fibres are surrounded by thin, glue-like sheets called connective tissue which fix the fibres to the bone, allowing them to move with the animal. The harder the muscle is worked, the more the connective tissue bulks up and consequently the tougher the meat will be. Fat, which provides energy and insulation, is interspersed within the connective tissue and under the skin of the animal. Fat contributes to the tenderness of meat, too, by lubricating the muscle fibres, making them taste more succulent and juicy.

The human body is capable of breaking down most meat – our teeth can break the fibres apart and our intestines digest them – but the eating process is far more enjoyable if the meat has good flavour and texture.

Meat and farming

Humans have been farming animals for their meat for thousands of years. As breeds of cattle, pigs and sheep have grown and diversified, so too has the choice of meat available to the consumer.

Methods of farming livestock can vary greatly. The way an animal is farmed for its meat depends on the individual farmer or organisation, which in turn controls the environment the animals are exposed to. Farming has seen the introduction of chemicals in the form of pesticides and fertilizers that are used to control the land and optimize yields. Intensive livestock farming – where stock is high and animals are kept in close confines – often means the animals will require chemical-based medicines to prevent infection and disease.

This type of farming may produce animals that become bored or aggressive, which can affect the meat quality.

Some farmers and organisations choose to farm organically. Organic farming is monitored by strict regulations to which farmers are bound to adhere in order to maintain their organic status. It uses natural substances and techniques for managing the land, such as introducing natural predators to control pests. Organic farming is viewed as being kinder

to the environment and to human health, because
organic produce is free from the chemical residues
that can be found in non-organic crops and meat.

Ultimately, the best-quality farmed meat comes
from healthy animals that have been well reared
from the day they were born until the moment
they are slaughtered.

Slaughtering animals for their meat is usually
carried out in a packing plant or harvesting facility.
In the developed world, animal slaughter practice
requires that animals be stunned before slaughter so
that their suffering is lessened, because death occurs
while the animal is unconscious. Once stunned, the
neck arteries are severed and the excessive bleeding
which ensues causes death by lack of oxygen to the
brain. In the case of most halal and kosher slaughter
practices, animals are not stunned before slaughter.

Besides cattle, pigs and sheep, other animals
slaughtered for their meat include horses, donkeys
and goats and kids. Horse meat is lean and densely
textured and the carcass is cut up in much the same
way as a cow's. Donkey meat is generally tough. It
requires grinding down or slow cooking in moist heat
and is typically used in stews and in sausage. Goat –
known as kid when the animal is slaughtered young
– has a similar flavour to lamb and beef. It is often
stewed, made into curries or barbecued.

Meat and health benefits

There are many positive reasons to include meat in your diet.
Lean meat is high in protein and contains all the essential
amino acids your body needs for energy, growth and repair.

Lean beef, for example, contains high levels of iron, essential for the production of haemoglobin, which transports oxygen in the blood around the body. The iron content varies according to the different types and cuts but generally the redder the meat, the higher the iron content. Beef and lamb can contain up to three times as much iron as pork and a darker cut of pork from the shoulder will contain more iron than a paler piece from the loin.

Meat also contains zinc, which keeps the reproductive system healthy and plays a part in wound-healing. Vitamin B12 is present in meat – in particularly high amounts in beef and liver – and is essential for the development of red blood cells to prevent anaemia and to protect the central nervous system.

However, eating meat should be part of a balanced diet. While its exact make-up varies according to the animal, its breed and how it was reared, meat can be high in saturated fat and has sometimes been linked to high blood pressure, bowel cancer and heart disease. If you are concerned about the fat content in meat, choose lean cuts and cook them on a roasting rack or ridged pan to allow excess fat to drain away.

The colour of meat

Many factors, including the species of the animal, its diet, exercise and age when slaughtered, as well as how the meat was processed and packaged, contribute to the colour of meat. Colour can be a reliable indicator of quality, yet brightly coloured meat – while pleasing to the eye – does not necessarily guarantee freshness or flavour.

Beef

Beef should be deep red, not bright crimson. A brownish tinge or deeper brown colour might suggest it has been aged. The longer meat is aged, the darker and more tender it will become. Fat should be creamy in colour and visible bones should be pink. Flecks of fat – known as marbling – should run through the meat. Cuts of beef or lamb without marbling may lack flavour or moisture once cooked.

Lamb

Lamb should be pale pinkish-brown. It should not be bloody or grey. The younger the animal, the paler and more tender the meat will be. Meat from sheep that are older, or have enjoyed more exercise during their lifetime, will be darker in colour. Fat around the edges should be creamy white, firm and slightly crumbly with no yellow colour at all. There should also be a fine marbling of fat through the meat, though less than you would find in a cut of beef. The bones in lamb cuts should be pink; a good example of this is lamb rib bones, named 'cherry ribs' for their distinctive colour. White bones indicate less tender meat from an older animal.

Pork

Pork should be pale pink and free from blood. Cuts that are too pale often become dry and stringy, and pork that is too dark will be tough though very juicy. Yellow or brown stains on the skin indicate poor-quality pork. Any small bones should be pinkish-blue in colour. White, brittle bones indicate a much older animal with substantially tougher meat. The meat should be covered with a thin, even layer of dense, milk-white fat, and any skin should be thin and ideally without hair. Pork cuts may have marbled fat, but pork from a young animal (pale grey-pink) will be juicy and tender without the need for it.

The texture of meat

The texture of meat can vary as much as its flavour. Tough steaks and chewy chops might taste great but they are rarely a pleasure to eat. So what makes some cuts more tender than others? First, some cuts of meat are naturally tougher than others – usually those taken from the parts of the animal that are nearer the ground and therefore work the hardest. These cuts contain more connective tissue and require slow cooking in moist heat or liquid to tenderise them.

The way the animal was reared and slaughtered and its meat processed and stored all contribute to the overall texture of the meat. The age of the animal is another factor that affects tenderness. Meat is made up of muscle fibres that increase in diameter as the animal ages. Therefore, a cut of meat from an older animal will be tougher and more fibrous than the same cut from a younger animal.

The way you prepare and cook meat will further influence its texture. A tough cut that is cooked quickly over a high heat will remain tough. Cook the same cut slowly in liquid over a low heat and the tough fibres and connective tissue will break down and tenderise. You can also improve the way you perceive the texture of meat by carving it across the grain, which reduces the length of the muscle fibres and makes the meat feel less chewy in the mouth.

When raw, all meat should feel firm and springy to the touch. The best cuts contain no gristle – a tough, inedible tissue – between the meat and the fat. Gristle is normally associated with older animals and can spoil the experience of chewing and the way the meat feels in the mouth.

Fat

Fat, which is described as being either saturated (solid at room temperature) or unsaturated (soft at room temperature), is one of the naturally occurring components of meat. We are often told that eating too much saturated animal fat is bad for us. However, when it comes to cooking, fat provides flavour and is essential for improving the texture of meat. Top fat – the layer under the skin that lies along the outside of a roast or steak – naturally bastes the meat by melting into it as it cooks. If you score through the top fat on a belly of pork or pork shoulder, you will be rewarded with succulent, flavoursome meat and the most pleasingly crisp crackling.

As well as a layer of top fat, red meat should also contain small flecks of the creamy white fat known as marbling. This fatty network breaks down during cooking, basting and tenderizing the meat as it does so, adding flavour and enhancing the eating quality. Meat that contains little or no marbling can taste tough, dry and flavourless because the muscle fibres shrink and contract when cooked, squeezing out their moisture, rather than being basted in melting fat. For this reason, it is always advisable to choose red meat that has some of this marbling within the flesh, even if it also has an outside layer of top fat.

Lard is a white fat from pork used in slow-cooking and deep-frying, particularly in Europe and China.

The term larding refers to a technique whereby firm strips of pork or beef fat are threaded into a lean roast using special needles. These fatty strips behave in a similar way to natural marbling and melt into the meat as it cooks, tenderising and flavouring it.

Other animal fats include suet, a hard, white beef fat taken from the kidneys that is used in pastries, dumplings and puddings. Dripping is the melted fat from a roast of meat, usually beef, which solidifies when cold. It can be reused in cooking or is traditionally spread on bread and sprinkled with salt and eaten cold.

Processing a carcass

Once slaughtered, meat must undergo certain processing techniques before it is ready for sale and consumption. Immediately after slaughtering, the flesh is still warm and too soft to be eaten. Rigor mortis then sets in and the muscles contract and stiffen. Meat taken from a carcass during this time would be incredibly tough. When rigor mortis wears off, around 24 hours after slaughtering, the animal carcass can then be hung to age or broken down into large cuts, known as primals.

Cutting up a carcass is a specialist skill and how it is carried out varies worldwide. The way a beef carcass is broken down in France, for example, is somewhat more intricate than other countries' methods. These days, most carcasses are broken down into retail cuts and packaged at the processing plant, rather than being delivered whole to butchers.

Ultimately, the purpose of butchery is to produce recognisable cuts for the butcher or retailer and, in turn, for the professional or home cook. Good butchery should minimise waste, thereby making the consumption of meat economical to everyone involved and respectful to the animal.

Ageing meat

The taste and texture of meat – particularly that of beef and lamb – can be improved by ageing. The ageing process allows the fibres of the meat to break down and soften, enhancing the final flavour and the eating quality of the meat. Ageing gives beef its characteristic gamey flavour and minimises the metallic taste it can sometimes have. However, due to time and money constraints, not all meat is aged sufficiently, and sometimes not at all.

Ageing is achieved by two methods: wet-ageing and dry-ageing. With wet-ageing, cuts of meat are sealed in vacuum packs ready for retail, allowing them to mature in their own blood. This process is more incidental than by design, as the meat can age during transport and storage. Meat that is wet-aged loses no moisture and its final weight – and consequently its retail value – remains unchanged. Because of this, wet-ageing is the cheaper and preferred option of many retailers, although some would argue that ageing meat in its own blood while sealed in packs is neither effective nor desirable.

Meat can also be aged by hanging – a process often referred to by supermarkets as dry-ageing. This is a slower process, taking up to four weeks, whereby the animal carcass, or cuts from it, is hung from hooks in a temperature-controlled environment. During hanging, the carcass undergoes a slow chemical change. As it dries out, the enzymes break down, tenderising and concentrating the flavours of the flesh. The hanging or dry-ageing process reduces the carcass's original weight by up to 20 per cent, due to moisture loss. It is an expensive process, as the meat must be stored during hanging before it can be packed and distributed. Dry-ageing does, however, produce more flavourful and tender meat than the wet-ageing process.

Whether meat is wet-aged or hung, its flavour and texture will be superior to meat that has been rushed through the processing chain and onto supermarket shelves without allowing it a chance to mature at all.

A good butcher

Where you choose to buy your meat can come down purely to convenience. You may head to your nearest supermarket or you might prefer to go out of your way to a meat specialist who offers what you consider to be the best product and service. Wherever you buy your meat, there are a few visual clues that can speak volumes about the quality of the meat a particular establishment has to offer.

First, the windows, walls and floor of the shop should be clean; if the visible public areas are dirty and unkempt, the state behind the scenes could well be worse. The meat should look fresh and appetising. It should be displayed attractively and within its own type – for example beef, pork and lamb should not be mixed together – and cuts should be labelled with detailed information. Meat should be shiny without being wet or slimy and have a light, fresh scent; avoid anything with a strong odour.

An advantage of buying meat from a butcher is that less – or none – of the meat is likely to be prepacked. A good butcher will be happy to share his knowledge of meat and be able to advise you. As he has been involved in buying or processing the meat himself, he is likely to be able to answer any questions about it. You can ask him to order in a particular cut or prepare a cut in a certain way – for example, to bone a leg of lamb, to score the fat on a belly of pork or to mince a piece of beef.

As well as asking for advice on which cuts to buy for a particular way of cooking or for a recipe, feel free to ask questions before you buy, including the following:

• whether the meat is organic or free-range

• how fresh the meat is – when the animal was slaughtered

• for how long the meat has been aged.

Packaging

Most meat on supermarket shelves is already pre-prepared and packaged. Packaging technology has come a long way since our grandparents', or even our parents', day. It is rare, though a delight, to find a traditional butcher, who still wraps meat loosely in brown, or 'butcher's', paper.

Packaging is designed to be practical and, in the absence of a butcher on hand to answer queries, it should also provide sufficient information about its contents: the kind of meat and the cut it is, the use-by date, the price per kilogram and the weight and price of the pack is the minimum information you should expect to see.

The traditional butcher might condemn the practice of vacuum-packing meat as being the worst kind of packaging there is, as the meat sits in a bloody marinade, sweating in its own juices and unable to 'breathe'. Breathing is important for meat because it allows the air to carry away excess moisture and the flavours to develop further. However, because vacuum-packing seals in the meat, it is considered to be one of the safest and most hygienic types of packaging. Vacuum-packed meat is convenient for retailers and consumers too, because it is easy to handle and transport.

If you buy vacuum-packed meat, remove it from the packaging and pat it dry with some kitchen towels. Rewrap it in brown paper or transfer it to a plate and cover loosely with cling film – bearing in mind that you will need to use it sooner than the specified date on the original packaging. If you are buying meat to use straight away, dry it off as soon as possible and allow it to breathe and come up to room temperature before cooking.

Another form of meat packaging is Controlled Atmosphere Packaging (CAP) and Modified Atmosphere Packaging (MAP). Meat is sealed in disposable containers with a mixture of gases, including oxygen, carbon dioxide and nitrogen, which act as preservatives. Like vacuum-packing, this technique allows the meat to be easily transported and prolongs its shelf life.

Hygiene

If you prepare or cook meat, a basic knowledge of food hygiene is important for safeguarding your health. By following a few simple steps you can drastically reduce any risk of food poisoning. The most common cause of food poisoning is pathogenic bacteria which can thrive on raw food, and particularly on raw and cooked meat and meat products such as stews, gravies and stocks.

Food poisoning is, at best, unpleasant, causing nausea, abdominal pain, vomiting and diarrhoea; for high-risk groups – the very young, the elderly, those with weakened immune systems and pregnant women – food poisoning can be life-threatening.

• Meat should be kept chilled between 1 and 5°C (34 and 41°F). Bringing meat up to room temperature before cooking is fine provided it does not sit around for longer than necessary.

• Before preparing and handling meat, wash hands thoroughly and wash again between handling different types of meat. Always handle meat with utensils rather than hands.

• Raw and cooked meats should be prepared separately with clean knives and never on the same cutting board.

• Keep meat out of the 'danger zone' temperature of 5–63°C (41–145°F), where bacteria multiply most rapidly. When heating or cooling food, particularly meat, do so as quickly as possible.

• Always check packaging for advice regarding storage and preparation. Don't be tempted to use meat which has passed its use-by date.

• Ensure your refrigerator is clean and that any spillages are wiped up immediately with a sanitised cloth.

• Although beef can be eaten raw, it is advisable to cook at least the outside surface of a steak or roast in order to kill most bacteria. Beef that is cooked medium-rare will have an internal (core) temperature of 60–70°C (140–160°F).

- Lamb should be cooked until at least medium-rare – that is, until at least slightly pink and without blood – with a core temperature of 55–60°C (130–140°F).

- Pork should be cooked until well done with a minimum core temperature of 75°C (170°F).

- Cool, cover and chill leftover meat as quickly as possible.

- Always reheat meat and meat dishes until piping hot with a core temperature of 70°C (160°F) for at least two minutes. Never reheat meat more than once.

- If you plan to eat anything that has come in contact with raw meat, such as a marinade, it must be heated to at least 75°C (170°F) before consumption. Never reuse marinades that have been in contact with meat.

Storing meat at home

- Put meat in the refrigerator as soon as you come home
  from shopping.

- Cooked meat should be cooled, then wrapped or covered before
  being chilled or frozen.

- Before chilling or freezing raw meat, rinse off any blood and pat it
  dry. Wrap in plastic film or put into a sealed container and refrigerate
  between 1 and 5°C (34 and 41°F) or freeze at -18°C (0°F) or colder.

- Always thaw meat in the refrigerator, not at room temperature.

- Roasts (raw or cooked) will last in the refrigerator for three to five
  days. Smaller cuts, such as steaks and chops (raw or cooked), will
  last for two to four days (vacuum-packed meat will last longer –
  refer to packaging instructions).

- Never allow food to go mouldy or rotten in the refrigerator.

Refrigerator know-how

When it comes to storing food, the key point to remember is to keep raw meat away from other food. All food, particularly raw and cooked meat, should be wrapped and placed in a dish or a sealed container before being chilled.

Top shelf

Vegetables and salad (salad crispers at the bottom of the refrigerator are commonly used but salad should ideally be stored above any raw meat)

In the door

Condiments and preserves (where the temperature fluctuates the most)

Middle shelf

Cooked meat and meat products, such as cured meat

Bottom shelf

Raw meat

Very bottom shelf

Raw poultry (the coldest spot)

Utensils for cooking meat

It is better to have a few well-chosen, good-quality utensils than a stack of cheaper ones that you are less likely to use. This list provides an idea of useful equipment for all levels of cooking, but there is no reason to rush out and buy everything at once – you can add to your collection over time. The symbols below indicate who is most likely to benefit from having each item.

Butcher

Professional chef

Home cook

Boning or meat-cutting table

Traditional work surface used by butchers to break a carcass down into cuts

Metal-mesh apron and gloves

For full protection against blades and other sharp objects

Bone saw

For sawing through bones when breaking down a carcass

Cleaver

For chopping up large pieces of meat efficiently and quickly

Mincer

For breaking down pieces of meat into minced meat

Electric meat slicer

For slicing meat quickly, efficiently and safely

Paring knife, cook's knife, boning knife

You are more likely to cut yourself with a blunt knife because of
the extra force required, so keep knives sharp

Sharpening steel or stone

Essential for keeping knives sharp

Wood, plastic or nylon colour-coded cutting boards

Whatever the type of board, always wash thoroughly with hot
soapy water immediately after use

Additional useful equipment

- Spatula or palette knife

  For turning or lifting meat during cooking

- Carving board with spikes

  For holding meat in place during carving

- Carving knife and fork

  For steadying and carving meat as efficiently and
  safely as possible

- Poultry shears

  For trimming fat and cutting through small bones

- Meat thermometer

  For checking doneness of meat and core temperatures

- Meat tenderiser

  For batting out tougher pieces of meat before cooking

- Skewers

  To test for doneness and for holding pieces of meat in place

- Baster

  For distributing fat and juices over meat as it cooks

- Pastry brush

  For brushing over oil and marinades
- String or silicone bands

  For tying up cuts of meat before roasting
- Long-handled tweezers

  For removing small, awkward bones
- Conical gravy strainer

  For removing lumps in gravy before serving
- Covered pot

  For roasting pieces of meat
- Casserole

  For cooking pot-roasts, braises and stews
- Selection of sturdy deep and shallow roasting tins

  Choose tins that can be used on the hob as well as in the oven
- Heavy frying pan

  Ideally cast-iron or one that can be used in the oven as well as
  on the hob
- Selection of heavy saucepans with lids

  For stocks, sauces and accompaniments; heavy bases provide even
  heat distribution

Tenderising meat

Some cuts of meat are naturally more tender than others.
Tougher cuts require tenderising before they can be enjoyed.

This can be done in a number of ways:

- By slow cooking in moist heat or liquid, either by poaching, pot-roasting, stewing or braising. This breaks down the muscle fibres and connective tissue.

- By pounding. Pounding with a meat tenderiser or rolling pin changes the composition of the muscle fibres, making the meat more tender. For ease, cover the meat in a layer of cling film or greaseproof paper before bashing it flat.

- By mincing. Mincing breaks down the connective tissue and any tough fibres in the meat, making it feel more tender in the mouth.

- By marinating. A marinade is a flavoured liquid that usually contains an acid, such as wine, lemon juice or vinegar, combined with aromatic and fragrant flavours, such as fresh or dried herbs, crushed or whole spices, garlic, ginger or sugar. Submerging meat in an acid-based marinade before cooking adds flavour and softens the muscle fibres of the meat. A marinade should be a balance of flavours that enhance and complement, rather than overpower, the flavour of the meat.

Marinades

A marinade may be cooked before it is applied to the meat. Cooking a marinade – for example, dissolving sugar in the liquid – allows its ingredients to meld together and become syrupy, helping it to coat the meat. A cooked marinade must be cooled before adding the meat.

Use non-metallic dishes when marinating because metals can react with the acid in the marinade. Turn the meat regularly to coat it evenly in the marinade. Alternatively, use a resealable plastic food-safe bag, which will allow the marinade to penetrate fully into the meat.

The length of time the meat is left in the marinade will depend on its size and cut. The longer the meat marinates, the softer its fibres will become and the more it will take on the flavours of the marinade. Smaller pieces of meat will soak up the marinade more quickly than larger cuts. Tough stewing cuts, such as chuck, can be marinated in the refrigerator for up to three days. A naturally tender cut of meat – such as beef fillet – requires only brief marinating to enhance the flavour.

The marinade liquid may also be added to the pan with the meat, provided it is brought up to the boil before serving. If the marinade is not required in the dish, the meat should be lifted from it and patted dry before cooking.

Preparing meat for roasting

To prepare a boneless or bone-in roast

Preheat the oven. Put the meat on a board and pat it dry with kitchen towel. Using a sharp knife or scissors, trim away any excess fat.

Weigh the meat and calculate the cooking time. Allow around 175g (6oz) meat per person for a boneless roast; 225g (8oz) for a bone-in roast.

Heat a roasting tin over a medium heat. Season the roast with salt and pepper and carefully add to the tin, fat-side down. If the cut of meat is lean or contains no top fat, you may need to add a little oil to the pan first. Quickly sear or brown the roast all over, turning with spoons or tongs. Remove from the tin.

Put a rack into the roasting tin and sit the browned roast on top. Transfer to a preheated oven to roast (see Roasting, page 45). Roasting fattier meats, such as pork and lamb, on a trivet set within the roasting tin allows excess fat to drain away.

You may wish to skip the searing step and roast the meat at a higher temperature for the first 20 minutes (see cooking times on page 45).

To stuff and tie a boneless roast

A boned roast of beef, pork or lamb can be opened out, stuffed and rolled before roasting to add extra texture and flavour.

Place the roast on a board and trim away any excess fat with a sharp knife or scissors. Lay the roast fat-side down on the board and open it out flat (cut the meat open with a knife if necessary).

Spoon over the stuffing in an even layer.

Roll up the meat to enclose the stuffing, so the fat is on the outside. Tie with string at evenly spaced intervals.

Slash the layer of top fat with a sharp knife, then season with salt and pepper.

Put the meat on a rack in a roasting tin and transfer it to a preheated oven to roast.

Cooking techniques

We cook meat to make it safe to eat and easier to digest, and to improve its flavour and texture. Applying heat alters its texture and colour. As red meat cooks, it changes from a deep red colour to a paler pink and through to a grey-brown. Its fibres contract and the water and juices within are squeezed out.

Before cooking meat, remove it from the refrigerator to let it come up to room temperature. This will help it cook evenly and ensure that the calculated cooking times will be accurate.

Roasting

Roasting is a method of cooking in the oven that requires high heat and a little fat. Basting meat – coating it with hot fat from the pan – is necessary if the meat is lean, though if the meat has a top layer of fat and good marbling the fat will melt into the meat as it cooks and basting will not be essential.

Roasting is best suited to tender cuts of meat that will cook relatively quickly and are not dried out by high heat. Slow roasting at a lower temperature can make some cuts of meat more succulent and tender. Tougher cuts, which contain more connective tissue, will require roasting for longer at a lower temperature.

The table below is a guide to the fastest way of roasting boneless cuts without compromising the meat's succulence. Weight for weight, a boneless roast will take longer to cook than a bone-in roast, as bones conduct heat and speed up the cooking time.

MEAT	CUTS SUITABLE FOR ROASTING	METHOD
Beef	Sirloin, fillet and rib	*Preheat the oven to 220°C (425°F). Brown the meat for 20 minutes, then reduce the temperature to 160°C (325°F) and roast for an additional 15 minutes per 450g (1lb) for rare, 20 minutes per 450g (1lb) for medium and 30 minutes per 450g (1lb) for well done.*
Pork	Loin, leg and shoulder	*Pork is usually cooked until the meat is well done. Preheat the oven to 220°C (425°F). Brown the meat for 20 minutes, then reduce the temperature to 190°C (375°F) and roast for an additional 25 minutes per 450g (1lb), plus 25 minutes at the end of the calculated time.*
Lamb	Loin, leg and shoulder	*Lamb is traditionally cooked until pink or rosy inside. Preheat the oven to 220°C (425°F). Brown the meat for 20 minutes, then reduce the temperature to 190°C (375°F) and continue roasting for 20 minutes per pound for pink. For well-done lamb, roast for an additional 20 minutes at the end of the calculated time.*

Frying

Frying is a fast method of cooking in a pan. It is ideal for small, tender cuts of meat, such as chops, cutlets and steaks.

Use a wide, uncovered pan. Oil the pan and preheat it until it is hot and the oil is rippling before adding the meat. Do not allow the oil to smoke in the pan because it will scorch the meat when it is added.

Pat the meat dry with kitchen towel before adding it to the pan, otherwise it will not brown and caramelise sufficiently.

Fry the meat in batches if the pan is not big enough. Overcrowding the pan will lower the cooking temperature and result in the meat becoming tough and dry.

The cooking time with frying depends more on the thickness of the meat than on its weight.

Char-grilling

This is a method of cooking meat quickly over a high heat in a shallow, ridged, cast-iron griddle pan to achieve either blackened diagonal lines or a criss-cross effect on both sides of the meat. It is a relatively healthy way of cooking meat, as it requires minimal additional cooking oil and any excess fat from the meat can drain away.

Before adding the meat, the pan is heated over a high heat and brushed with oil to keep the meat from sticking. During cooking, the meat can be brushed with a marinade or extra oil if it is looking dry.

Stir-frying

Stir-frying is a fast way of cooking strips, cubes or slices of meat in a round or flat-bottomed wok or large frying pan. The oil is heated in the pan until hot and rippling and the meat – often marinated for extra flavour – is then added and cooked quickly over a high heat, while being moved around constantly with a spatula.

Once seared, the meat can be removed from the pan. Chopped vegetables, a marinade and any other ingredients can then be added and cooked quickly before the meat is returned to the pan to heat through and mingle with the flavours.

Because stir-frying is such a fast method of cooking, having all the ingredients ready-prepared and close to hand before you start cooking is vital – there will be little time for chopping once cooking begins.

Grilling

Grilling is a method of cooking whereby direct heat is applied from above.

Just as preheating the oven is essential before roasting meat, it is important to preheat the grill to its highest setting before adding the meat. A strong heat will help to give the meat a lovely caramelised flavour.

Ideally, grilled meat should be slightly charred and crisp on the outside and succulent and juicy within. Only fairly thin, tender cuts are suitable for grilling and they should be brushed with a little oil or melted butter first.

Browning and searing

Browning meat in hot oil at a high temperature before cooking it more slowly enhances its flavour and appearance. Browning is often necessary for cubes, slices and strips of meat destined for stews, pot-roasts and braises. Searing usually refers to browning a roast. Browning or searing in a hot pan on the hob or at a high temperature in the oven will caramelise the outside of the meat and seal in its juices. Sometimes a recipe will require dusting the meat in flour before browning; the addition of this starch will thicken any liquid added to the pan later, turning it into a rich sauce.

Braising

For a braise, the meat is first browned with a combination of finely diced vegetables such as carrots, celery and onion, known as a 'mirepoix', in a casserole or heavy pot on the hob or in the oven. Stock or another flavoursome liquid is then added and the dish is covered with a tight-fitting lid. Braises are made with meat which is reasonably lean and rich in connective tissue. During cooking the vegetables break down and, along with the natural gelatines released from the meat, thicken the liquid, resulting in a deliciously sticky sauce. As liquid is required, braising is more like a stew than a pot-roast. Using a good-quality stock will give the braise an intense depth of flavour.

Poaching

Simmering meat gently in boiling liquid on the hob or in the oven is known as poaching. It is suitable for cooking both tender and tougher cuts. The liquid should not be allowed to come to a vigorous boil because this will cause the meat to disintegrate. Take care not to overcook the meat, because it will dry out and become fibrous. It is common to flavour the cooking water with vegetables and herbs, such as chopped onions, carrots, bay leaves and a bouquet garni or herb bundle; this flavoured liquid can then be served as a broth or as part of the finished dish.

Pot-roasting

Pot-roasting is similar to braising, except that it does not require stock or liquid other than the cooking fat, although in some instances a little additional liquid is used. It is therefore a drier method of cooking than braising, relying on the meat's own juices to provide moisture. The term 'roasting' is confusing, because the meat is not so much roasted as baked in a casserole dish or heavy pot with a tight-fitting lid on the hob or in the oven. Meat used for pot-roasting is usually fattier than that for braising and the result should taste roasted.

The meat is first browned, then cooked on a mirepoix of diced vegetables with the cooking fat and sometimes a little stock or liquid. The meat should fit snugly into the dish; if the dish is too roomy, the meat is likely to dry out. Pot-roasting is a great way of tenderising tougher cuts. The diced vegetables can be served with the meat or broken down and used in an accompanying sauce.

Stewing

For a stew, meat is cut into cubes and browned before being simmered on the hob or in the oven in plenty of liquid, such as stock, water, beer or wine. The cooking liquid forms part of the finished dish and, towards the end of cooking, can be thickened with flour, cornflour or a paste of butter and flour (*beurre manié*) to form a gravy-like sauce. Chopped onions, mushrooms and carrots can be added with the meat to provide extra colour, texture and flavour. This moist slow-cooking method is ideal for tenderising tougher cuts of meat; cuts with a generous amount of connective tissue and marbling make for the best stews. Take care not to overcook the stew, because the meat will disintegrate or become stringy. White stews are made without browning the meat first; as a result, the finished stew is paler in colour.

Spit-roasting

A whole animal carcass – usually a pig or a sheep – may be spit-roasted over an open fire. This is a great way of feeding a crowd and is something of a celebratory meal. The carcass is mounted and tied with wire onto the spit, then rubbed or brushed with oil. With pork, the skin is first scored all over and rubbed with salt (this will produce the most delicious crackling). The spit and carcass are then suspended above burning embers and turned at intervals to allow the meat to become an even golden brown. After this initial browning process, the spit is moved further away from the heat to let the meat to cook slowly and evenly while the spit turns. The natural flavours of the meat are sealed within and are enhanced by the aroma of the burning embers. To ensure that the meat roasts evenly, it is necessary to allow time for the carcass to come up to room temperature before being spit-roasted – this can take 12 hours or longer depending on its size.

Stocks

Stocks are clear, deeply flavoured liquids used for stews, soups, gravies, braises and sauces. They are quick to prepare, and just require some time to bubble away. A brown stock is made from beef, lamb or pork bones. It is richly flavoured and deeply coloured because the raw meat bones are first roasted until they are golden and caramelised. Any meat clinging to the bones will add extra flavour to the stock.

The roasted bones are then fully immersed in a pan of cold water with a selection of chopped vegetables, such as leek, carrot, onion, celery and herbs, such as parsley stalks, thyme and bay leaves. The liquid is brought to the boil and simmered for several hours until it takes on the rich flavour of the bones and other ingredients and has sufficiently reduced in volume; stocks are thickened by reduction, not by adding flour. As the stock simmers, any fat rising to the surface should be skimmed off with a spoon. Use stocks in the same meat dishes as the bones from which they have been made. A good stock will taste flavourful enough to be enjoyed on its own as a broth.

Gravy

Gravy is a popular accompaniment to roasted meats. It is traditionally made from the pan juices given out by the meat as it cooks. After cooking, the roast or pieces of meat are lifted from the pan and kept warm while the gravy is prepared. Excess fat is removed from the pan, leaving any brown juices and caramelised bits from the meat; these add plenty of flavour.

The pan is returned to the hob and a small quantity of liquid, such as wine or water, is stirred into the flavoursome juices (this is known as 'deglazing'). Stock is gradually stirred in – the type of stock should match the meat that the gravy will be served with – the liquid is brought to a simmer and allowed to reduce until slightly thickened. Some gravies are thickened by stirring a little flour into the meat juices and letting it cook for a few minutes before the stock is added. The flavour of gravy can be enhanced by additional ingredients, such as redcurrant jelly and fresh herbs.

Carving

Carving is the process of slicing roasted meat into portions before serving. The cooked roast is removed from the pan, covered loosely with foil and left in a warm place for up to half an hour. This is known as resting, and it allows the juices to redistribute throughout the meat, ensuring it is succulent before carving.

The meat should then be transferred to a carving board, ideally one with spikes to hold the underside of the joint in place. Use a carving fork in one hand to steady the roast, and slice pieces of meat from the joint with a sharp carving knife. Boneless roasts are easier to carve than those containing a bone or several bones, which require a certain amount of skill to cut around in order to release the meat.

Accompaniments

Various sauces and accompaniments have become popular to serve with meat. Many accompaniments are now sold readymade in jars and packets but it is easy – and often more rewarding in terms of flavour and cost – to make your own. Whether you buy or make your accompaniments, their purpose should be the same: to enhance and complement the flavour of the meat with which they are served.

Some traditional accompaniments

• **Horseradish sauce for roast beef**
For the best, most pungent flavour, use freshly grated horseradish mixed with a generous amount of lightly whipped cream or crème fraîche. Season with salt and pepper and a little sugar to taste.

• **Apple sauce for roast pork**
Cook peeled, sliced apples in a pan with a splash of water and a squeeze of lemon juice until softened and breaking up. Beat in a little sugar and butter until the sauce is thick and smooth. Best served warm.

• **Mint sauce for roast lamb**
Put some freshly chopped mint leaves into a heatproof bowl. Cover with boiling water and equal quantities of sugar and white wine vinegar. Mix well to dissolve the sugar, adding a little more of either sugar or vinegar to balance the flavours. Season and serve cold.

Preserving, curing and cold-smoking

Before commercial refrigeration, preserving was the only way of ensuring that meat and fish were free from decay and safe to eat. Cured meats provided essential nutrients for sailors at sea for months on end. Traditional curing uses salt to draw water from the meat, thereby reducing its volume, concentrating its flavour and lengthening its lifespan. Herbs, spices and sugar can be mixed with the salt for extra flavour. Today, a lot of commercially preserved meat has been cured using chemicals and flavourings, and the ancient technique of preserving or curing food at home has almost disappeared. Curing meat by injecting liquid – rather than extracting it – to bulk up its weight is not uncommon.

Traditional curing requires few ingredients – a good-quality piece of meat, salt, air and time. To cure meat at home, choose a wooden, plastic or ceramic container (avoid metal as it can react with the salt) and rub the meat – such as pork belly, pork leg or beef brisket – with handfuls of salt. Cover loosely, then store in a cool place, changing the salt every day for a week.

Wet-curing with brine is another way of preserving meat. A basic brine mix is three parts water to one part salt, to which herbs and spices can be added for extra flavour. Wine, beer or fruit juice can be used as part of the liquid quantity. The meat is submerged in the liquid, allowing it to release its water gradually, thereby concentrating its natural flavours and taking on the flavours of the brine.

After meat has been wet- or dry-cured, it is rinsed and can then be air-dried. This process can take up to several months and it allows the flavours of the meat to develop even further. Air-drying is a common practice for cured pork and beef, such as salami, Parma ham, bresaola and African biltong.

Cured beef, lamb and pork can also be cold-smoked. This is a slower process than hot-smoking and further preserves and intensifies the flavour of cured meat.

Cold-smoking requires a low heat (65°C/150°F or lower) and can be achieved in a smoking box, which resembles a small, covered oven filled with a layer of woodchips and containing a rack for the meat to sit on. Cold-smoking can also be achieved by hanging cured meat over a smouldering log fire. Smoked meats include beef jerky and bacon.

BEEF

Beef – the name of the meat taken from a bovine animal or carcass – is hugely popular all over the world. The carcass is broken down into cuts, known as primals, which can be categorised into three larger groups: middle meats, end meats and thin meats. Almost all parts of the animal are eaten. Beef is cooked and prepared in all sorts of ways, from simple grilling or frying to roasting and stewing; it can also be served raw, as in steak tartare or carpaccio.

Primal cuts

The primal cuts are those made in the initial stage of butchering. They may be sold whole, or subdivided into smaller cuts for sale to home cooks.

Chuck

Rib

Shank

Brisket

Chuck

The chuck is the largest of the eight primal cuts from the beef animal or carcass. It consists of the large section of shoulder and includes the first five ribs.

The chuck breaks down into two sub-primals: the chuck roll and the boneless shoulder clod in the lower portion. A sub-cut referred to as shoulder comes from the shoulder clod; most other sub-cuts come from the chuck roll. The blade is in the upper part of the chuck. Chuck can be divided into bone-in and boneless cuts for roasts and steaks and is often minced and used in hamburgers, and particularly in hamburger steaks, which are seasoned with chopped onion, shaped into a steak and fried or grilled and served with gravy and onions.

Flavour

This primal provides numerous economical cuts which are extremely flavourful. They contain plenty of connective tissue, which breaks down during cooking.

Cooking

To break down the connective tissue and tenderise the meat, chuck cuts demand long, slow cooking in liquid, such as pot-roasting and stewing.

Chuck-eye roast and steaks

The chuck-eye roast is a boneless cut from the centre of the chuck roll. It can be cut into steaks.

Flavour

This is a particularly tender cut of chuck with good flavour.

Cooking

The roast is best suited to braising or roasting until medium-rare. Steaks can be grilled or fried.

Also known as

Boneless chuck roll, Scotch tender, boneless chuck fillet, mock tender steak, boneless chuck steak, chuck tender steak and chingolo *(Spanish).*

Substitutes

Top blade roast, top blade steak.

Chuck pot-roast

This is a cut from the arm, shoulder or blade chuck and can be bone-in or boneless. Cuts from the chuck pot-roast are known as arm steaks and arm Swiss steaks.

Flavour

Chuck pot-roast has great flavour. It is usually well marbled and contains plenty of connective tissue.

Cooking

Chuck pot-roast requires long, slow cooking and is best suited to stewing, braising or pot-roasting.

Also known as

Bone-in roasts include arm pot-roast, blade roast, cross-rib pot-roast, shoulder roast and épaule (French). Boneless roasts include bolar roast, chuck-eye roast, arm roast, boneless cross rib, centre-cut chuck roast, Diamond Jim roast, top blade (flat-iron roast), shoulder clod roast, chuck roll and chuck wagon roast. Blade roast includes the top blade steak (flat-iron steak) and the under blade roast.

Chuck steak

This is a large boneless steak
from the chuck roll.

Flavour

*Chuck steak is a relatively
tough and chewy cut but it
has good flavour.*

Cooking

*It requires tenderising by
slow, moist cooking and is
best marinated before being
slowly braised.*

Substitute

Round steak.

Denver cut

This is a relatively new steak, popular in the US, cut from the chuck roll. It offers great value.

Flavour

Thanks to its superb marbling, Denver cut is incredibly tender and juicy.

Cooking

It can be marinated or seasoned with a rub before being grilled or fried.

7-bone pot roast

This economical cut from the shoulder clod takes its name from the shoulder blade bone contained within it. It can be cut into steaks. In the US it is one of the favourite cuts for pot roasts.

Flavour

The 7-bone pot roast requires long, slow cooking in liquid, such as stewing, braising or pot-roasting, to tenderise it.

Also known as

Centre cut pot-roast, chuck 7-bone roast, chuck roast centre cut and 7-bone roast.

Substitute

Arm roast.

Petite filet

This is a relatively new and popular cut. The petite filet is cut from the top of the shoulder and is similar to pork tenderloin in size and shape. Allow one piece to serve two people.

Flavour

The petite filet is sold ready trimmed, so it is lean yet naturally juicy.

Cooking

It can be roasted, grilled or cut into medallions and fried.

Also known as

Shoulder petite tender, shoulder tender roast and shoulder tender medallions.

Shoulder pot-roast and shoulder steaks

This is a boneless, economical cut from the shoulder clod. Shoulder steaks are cut from the shoulder pot-roast.

Flavour

The shoulder pot-roast can be incredibly flavoursome, if somewhat tough.

Cooking

It becomes meltingly tender with long, slow cooking and benefits from marinating before being braised.

Also known as

Shoulder roast.

Flavour

The shoulder centre has an excellent texture and flavour.

Cooking

It can be grilled, and often benefits from being marinated or braised.

Also known as

Clod heart and mock brisket. Steaks are known as beef filet and ranch-style steak, barbecue steak, cross-rib steak, full steak and shoulder clod steak.

Substitute

Sirloin.

Shoulder centre

Shoulder centre is a cheaper alternative to sirloin. It can be roasted whole or cut into steaks. Leftovers are great sliced cold in salads and sandwiches the next day.

Chuck boneless short ribs

Chuck boneless short ribs are almost square in shape. As they are cooked in liquid they are best eaten with a knife and fork rather than with fingers. They may consist of just the first five ribs cut across the bone or cut parallel to the bone.

Flavour

Boneless short ribs contain some fat and connective tissue.

Cooking

In order to become lovely and tender they require slow, moist cooking, such as braising.

Also known as

Chuck short ribs, boneless short ribs and boneless country-style beef chuck ribs.

Brisket

Brisket is one of the thin meats and is taken from the lower chest of the beef animal or carcass beneath the first five ribs. Brisket is an inexpensive boneless cut, weighing around 7.25kg (16lb), and is used to make commercial corned beef.

Flavour

Brisket can be incredibly flavoursome and tender if cooked slowly. For best results, choose well-marbled brisket.

Cooking

Brisket must be cooked slowly in moist heat, such as in a braise or pot-roast. It responds well to marinating and smoking (it is particularly popular for smoking on the barbecue). It is worth trimming off some fat before cooking but brisket will dry out and toughen if it is too lean.

Substitute

Bottom round roast.

Flat cut brisket

This is a large, lean, flat cut weighing up to 4kg.

Flavour

Flat cut brisket has great flavour and texture.

Cooking

It requires slow, moist cooking over a low heat and is therefore suitable for pot-roasting and braising.

Also known as

Deckle off, first cut, flat half, navel end brisket, thin cut, pecho (Spanish) and poitrine (French).

Point cut brisket

This is a smaller, fattier cut of brisket. It is triangular in shape.

Flavour

*Point cut brisket has more
flavour than flat cut brisket.*

Cooking

*Point cut brisket is best suited
to pot-roasting.*

Also known as

Point cut and deckle.

Rib

The rib primal weighs around 16kg (35lb) and is taken from the section of the animal's back lying between the chuck and the loin. The rib is one of the middle cuts of the beef animal or carcass and consists of ribs 6 to 12 and part of the backbone.

It also contains the rib-eye muscle, which runs through its centre. This muscle is barely exercised and is therefore incredibly tender. The rib is one of the most sought-after of all the primals and is therefore an expensive choice.

Flavour

Cuts from the rib are often dry-aged by quality butchers to produce an even richer flavour and tender texture.

Cooking

Cuts from the rib can be roasted, grilled or fried.

Wing rib and rib steaks

The wing rib is considered to be one of the best cuts of beef and includes between two and seven ribs. It is juicy, tender and well marbled and is an impressive roast to serve at the table. The term 'prime rib' refers to a wing rib in general and is not necessarily an indication of the quality. Rib steaks and chops are cut from the wing rib. If the meat is cut away to expose the bone, it is known as a Frenched rib chop.

Flavour

The wing rib contains plenty of fat marbling which breaks down and melts as it cooks, giving it an incredible texture and rich flavour.

Cooking

It is tender enough to be cooked by dry heat, such as roasting. A standing rib roast is roasted in a standing position with the ribs stacked vertically.

Also known as

Rib roast, bone-in rib-eye roast, fore rib, prime rib, rib-eye and rib-roast. Rib steaks are also known as beauty steak, cowboy steak, market steak, shell steak, Spencer steak and entrecôte (French).

Rib-eye roast and rib-eye steak

The rib-eye roast is a boneless cut that can be cut into rib-eye steaks. Both roast and steaks contain part of the tender rib-eye muscle.

Flavour

Rib-eye roast and steaks are well marbled, extremely succulent, tender and full of flavour.

Cooking

The rib-eye roast is best suited to roasting and braising.

Substitute

Fillet roast or rib roast.

Back ribs

Back ribs are the bones that are removed from a rib roast to make it a rib-eye roast. They are usually sold in slabs. If they are boned they are called boneless short ribs. The Royal Rib is the sixth rib on its own, partially cut from the bone, then rolled and tied.

Flavour

Back ribs are slightly fatty without a great deal of meat but tasty nonetheless.

Cooking

They are often marinated before cooking. They are best grilled or barbecued.

Also known as

Rib caps, rib bones, Texas ribs and rib lifters.

Substitute

Short ribs.

Hanger steak

The hanger steak is an interior cut which hangs from the last rib below the fillet. It is not technically classed under any primal; rather, it is its own individual cut. The hanger steak is often minced and used in burgers and is a popular cut in France.

Flavour

The hanger steak is packed with flavour.

Cooking

It should be cooked quickly over a high heat. It is often marinated before cooking to tenderise it.

Also known as

Hanging steak, hanging tender, bistro steak, boxeater steak, body skirt, onglet (French) and solomillo de pulmon (Spanish).

Substitute

Skirt steak or flank steak.

Forequarter and hindquarter flank

The forequarter and hindquarter flank are taken from the plate section of the beef carcass and are part of the thin meats.

The plate weighs around 14kg and is a continuation of the brisket primal. It continues to the flank, towards the rear underside of the animal. The flank weighs around 9kg. It is boneless and can be cut into steaks. The short plate is part of the upper part of the plate primal and is where the short ribs are taken from.

Flavour

The flanks can be relatively tough and are not generally considered to be a good cut for roasts.

Cooking

Flank is often used for minced beef or cut into strips for fajitas.

Skirt

Taken from the short plate, the skirt is long and thin. There is one on each side of the carcass and it can be divided into either the inside or the outside. The inside skirt is more desirable as it contains less of the membrane from the diaphragm.

Flavour

Skirt is well marbled and is particularly flavourful.

Cooking

Because of its loose texture and rich flavour, skirt responds well to marinating for up to 24 hours. It can then be grilled or fried, though care must be taken not to overcook it, which will toughen the meat. Skirt is traditonally used in Cornish pasties.

Also known as

Rump skirt, thin steak and Philadelphia steak.

Flank steak

This is a small, moderately priced boneless steak weighing up to 1kg (2lb). Strips of flank steak are often used in Mexican fajitas and in Asian cuisine.

Flavour

Flank steak is tougher than the loin or rib steaks but flavoursome nonetheless. To improve its tenderness it is often cut across the grain.

Cooking

It is best suited to being marinated, then grilled or fried until rare or medium-rare.

Also known as

Jiffy steak, bavetta (Italian) and bavette (French).

Substitute

Hanging tender or skirt steak.

Short ribs

Short ribs can be taken from any of the sections of 12 ribs, including those in the short plate. Ribs taken from here can be expensive but are more economical than chuck ribs.

Cooking

Short ribs can be braised, slow-roasted or boiled.

Also known as

Short plate ribs.

Flavour

They are tender and rich in flavour if cooked slowly in moist heat.

Substitute

Back ribs.

Loin

The loin primal is one of the middle meats of the beef animal or carcass and includes the thirteenth rib and backbone. It consists of the short loin and the strip loin.

The primal weighs around 18kg (40lb) and is taken from the area between the rib and sirloin primals. The quality of the loin – and particularly the marbling within it – is often used to gauge the grade of the entire animal. Loin cuts can be bone-in or boneless. They are expensive and are often kept for special occasions. The front portion of the smaller, pointed fillet lies parallel to the loin.

Flavour

Loin cuts can be incredibly tender and flavoursome, with a dense grain. Cuts with the most marbling are particularly succulent and tender – the loin can be a little chewy if the marbling is insufficient – and cuts from the rib end are generally the most tender. Whole loins are often dry-aged by hanging.

Also known as

Diamond cut, short loin, shell loin, short-cut beef, strip loin and top loin.

Cooking

To retain optimum texture and flavour the loin is best cooked rare or medium-rare. Loin roasts are roasted; steaks are best suited to frying or grilling.

Top loin steak

The top loin steak comes from the top of the loin section and can be bone-in or boneless.

Flavour

The top loin steak is tender and flavourful.

Cooking

It requires hot, fast cooking, such as frying or grilling. It is best served rare or medium-rare.

Also known as

New York strip steak, Ambassador steak, boneless club steak, hotel-style steak, Kansas City steak, strip loin steak, veiny steak, shell steak and faux filet *(French).*

T-bone steak
....

The T-bone steak is cut from the
front section of the loin, next to the
ribs. The steak includes a section of
the fillet and strip loin. It takes its
name from the T-shaped bone that
runs through the centre of the meat.

Flavour

*T-bone steak is incredibly
tender and flavourful.*

Cooking

*It is best fried or grilled until
rare or medium-rare.*

Also known as

Bistecca alla Fiorentina *in
Tuscany, where it is large
enough to be shared between
two people.*

Substitute

Porterhouse steak.

Flavour

*The porterhouse steak is tender
and full of flavour.*

Cooking

*It is best fried or grilled until
rare or medium-rare.*

Substitute

T-bone steak.

Porterhouse steak
....

The porterhouse steak is cut from the middle section of the loin.
Like the T-bone steak it contains the T-shaped bone, but it consists of a
larger section of the fillet and the strip loin and consequently commands
a higher price than the T-bone steak. There are strict guidelines as to
how large the fillet section of the steak must be for the steak to be
classed as porterhouse.

Fillet roast and steak

The fillet roast is cut from the long pointed section called the fillet, which lies alongside the loin. It is expensive but perceived as good value as there is little or no wastage. The roast ranks as number one in tenderness of all the cuts from the beef carcass. The roast can be cut into steaks or thinly sliced for the classic Italian dish, carpaccio.

Flavour

Because it is an inner muscle that is rarely worked or exercised, the fillet has a delicately mellow flavour and a meltingly tender texture.

Cooking

It requires minimal preparation, although some recipes call for it to be stuffed. It cooks quickly and can be fried, grilled or roasted. Fillet steaks can be grilled or fried.

Also known as

Filet steak, fillet of beef; bifteck, filet and filet mignon (French). Fillet steaks are also known as tournedos (French). A thick steak cut from here is known as Châteaubriand in France.

Chain

This is largely gristle which runs along the length of the fillet and has hardly any meat on it. It can sometimes be sold with the fillet. The chain can be cut into steaks and is fairly expensive but there is little or no wastage.

Flavour
Delicately flavoured.

Cooking
This is a versatile cut that can be roasted, fried or grilled.

Also known as
Rope, bavette *and* chaînette *(French).*

Sirloin

The sirloin primal is taken from the upper hip of the beef animal or carcass. It weighs around 10kg (22lb) and is one of the middle meats. It is less tender than the loin and rib primals and is therefore a cheaper cut.

The sirloin can be divided into the top sirloin – the stub end of the fillet – and the bottom sirloin. Sometimes part of the bottom sirloin can be included in the round primal, in which case it is known as the sirloin tip. Most cuts from the sirloin are full flavoured, although their texture can vary in terms of tenderness depending from where exactly in the primal they have been taken.

Flavour

The top sirloin is favoured over the bottom sirloin; it is worked less by the animal and is less tough. Cuts can be bone-in or boneless. A sirloin steak with fine, even marbling can sometimes be as tender as a fillet steak.

Cooking

Some sirloin cuts are suitable only for stewing or braising, while others offer tender steaks for flash-frying. Sirloin is also used for minced beef. Two sirloins roasted together (sometimes with the round) is known as a baron of beef.

Corner cut roast and steak

This is a curved, triangular-shaped cut taken from the bottom of the sirloin. It is boneless, relatively inexpensive, and offers excellent value for money as there is little wastage. Corner-cut steaks are cut from the corner-cut roast.

Flavour

The corner-cut roast contains little fat and can provide great tenderness and a robust flavour.

Cooking

It responds well to marinades and strong flavours. The roast can be grilled or roasted. Allow the top fat to melt into the meat as it roasts. Leftovers are great sliced and served cold in sandwiches the next day. Corner-cut steaks are great for barbecuing or frying.

Also known as

Tri-tip roast and tri-tip steak, knuckle cap, Santa Maria barbecue, sirloin triangle muscle, triangle roast and triangle tip. Corner-cut steaks are also known as triangle steaks.

Top sirloin roast

The top sirloin roast is usually sold boneless, though it can also be bone-in. It is more tender than the bottom sirloin as it is worked less by the animal, and is a great-value choice for feeding a crowd.

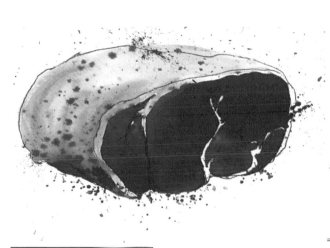

Flavour

Top sirloin roast is less expensive than a rib roast but just as impressive and flavourful.

Cooking

Roasting allows the top fat to melt over and baste the meat as it cooks.

Also known as

Centre cut sirloin roast, top sirloin butt, head loin, hip sirloin and coulotte (French).

Substitute

Rib-eye roast or rib roast.

Flavour

Great for grilling or frying.

Also known as

Petite top sirloin steak and sirloin butt steak. A thick-cut top sirloin steak is also known as Châteaubriand *(although in France the* Châteaubriand *is cut from the fillet).*

Top sirloin steak

This is a boneless steak cut from the top sirloin. Some top sirloin steaks can be mouth-wateringly juicy and full of flavour.

Round

Weighing around 36kg (80lb), the round is only slightly smaller than the chuck primal. It is one of the end meats and is taken from the top of the hind leg of the beef animal or carcass, continuing down towards the shank.

The round is divided into knuckle, top round and bottom round and contains a section of the aitchbone (hipbone). Cuts from certain parts of the round (including the sirloin) are known as rump. Beef rolls, beef olives, *involtini* (Italian) and *roulade* (French) are cut from the round. These are tough, thin cuts which are pounded, stuffed, rolled and then braised, usually in a rich sauce.

Flavour

Meat cut from the round is lean and not especially tender, particularly the parts closer to the ground, which are exercised more and are consequently tough.

Cooking

Round cuts are generally suited to slow, moist cooking methods, such as pot-roasting, which break down the connective tissue and bring out the flavour. Round can also be dried out and smoked to make beef jerky.

Top round

The top round is a lean roast from which thick steaks are cut.
It is cut from the upper, inner thigh and is therefore the most tender
part of the round.

Flavour

*The meat is lean and
densely textured.*

Cooking

*Top round is quite flavourful
but requires marinating before
cooking to tenderise it. It is
best suited to pot-roasting.*

Substitutes

Flank steak.

Flavour

*This can be a flavourful cut
if cooked correctly.*

Cooking

*Silverside demands slow,
moist cooking in order to
tenderise it and for the flavour
to be released. It is often cut
up for stewing and used as
kebab meat.*

Silverside

Silverside is the lowest part of the round cut. It is taken from the
outside of the leg and, as it is the most exercised, the meat is relatively
tough and contains a lot of connective tissue. The silverside, or bottom
round, can be further divided into eye of round, the flat and the heel.
Bottom round cuts are best braised or cooked slowly in liquid to
tenderise them. The heel is a boneless cut and is the toughest of all the
bottom round cuts. Cuts from the bottom round can be known as rump.

Also known as

*Manhattan roast and steak,
Gooseneck roast, Swiss steak
and breakfast steak.*

Pope's eye roast and steak

The Pope's eye, which sits in the middle of the round, is generally a tough cut.

Flavour

With correct cooking, this can be a deliciously flavourful cut.

Cooking

Pope's eye roasts and steaks require slow, moist cooking, such as braising or pot-roasting. Steaks benefit from being marinated before being grilled or braised.

Also known as

Eye of round, breakfast steak and sandwich steak.

Substitute

Round tip roast or round tip steak.

Flavour

Topside roast is less tough than roasts cut from other round cuts.

Cooking

It can be roasted but is often braised or cut up into stewing steak.

Also known as

Round tip roast and steak, ball tip roast and steak, trimmed tip steak (if the cut has been trimmed), sirloin tip steak, breakfast steak, knuckle steak, tip centre steak and round peeled knuckle.

Topside roast and steak

Topside steaks are cut from the topside roast.

Substitute

Pope's eye roast or steak.

Sirloin tip centre roast and sirloin tip centre steak

The sirloin tip centre is a simple, economical cut which makes a quick and easy roast, or may be made into stewing meat, cut into strips for stir-frying or minced.

Flavour

Lean and tender with good flavour.

Cooking

Benefits from marinating. Best suited to roasting, frying or grilling to medium-rare.

Sirloin tip side steak

This is a relatively new and economical steak. Although it is classed as part of the round, it is technically the very end of the sirloin.

Flavour

The sirloin tip side steak is a boneless, lean cut. It is less tender than the tip centre steak.

Cooking

It requires marinating before being grilled or fried.

Flavour

Meat from the knuckle is less tender than that from the sirloin but it has excellent flavour. The most tender part is the centre of the knuckle.

Cooking

The knuckle is best suited to roasting. Slightly tougher steaks cut from the knuckle are nevertheless tasty and are often cut into thin strips or slices.

Also known as

Sirloin butt roast, breakfast steak, minute steak and sandwich steak.

Knuckle

The knuckle is cut from the top of the round, just behind the sirloin. It is a versatile boneless cut that can be divided into roasts and steaks. Strips of meat for the Russian dish, Stroganoff, are often cut from the knuckle.

Shank

The shank primal is a basic cut that is taken from the fore or rear leg of the carcass and has a bone running through its centre. The rear shank is considered to be part of the round.

Flavour

Shank is a relatively lean cut and is really flavoursome. It is naturally tough with plenty of gelatinee-rich connective tissue. The rear shank has little culinary value as it is particularly tough.

Cooking

Fore and rear shanks can be cooked whole and are suitable for long, slow stewing to tenderise the meat. They can also be minced and used in processed meat products.

Also known as

The hind leg is known as leg of beef and the fore leg is known as shin.

Shank cross-cut

Shank cross-cut is cut across the shank and therefore contains a round piece of the leg bone in the centre.

Flavour

This is a rich and flavoursome cut.

Cooking

Shank cross-cuts require slow, moist cooking in liquid and are therefore ideal for stewing or simmering in a stock until the meat falls away from the bone. The stock can then be turned into a delicious beef soup, combined with the shredded meat.

Offal

Offal is cuts taken from the extremities of the animal or the organs within. They are also known as innards or variety meats.

Brains

Cows' brains are taken from the front of the skull. They are a popular delicacy in France, although following the BSE outbreak, they are no longer available in some countries. Cows' brains should be plump and firm. To prepare, soak in salted water then rinse and remove the membrane and any blood vessels. Poach whole or slice and fry in butter until tender and serve sprinkled with lemon juice and chopped herbs.

Tongue

A whole tongue from a beef carcass is long and flat and larger than you might imagine. To prepare, soak in water, then poach in a light stock until tender. Remove the tough, inedible skin before eating. Tongue is often served cold, usually jellied and pressed ready to be sliced.

Cheeks

Beef cheeks are taken from the cheek area of the head of the beef carcass. To prepare, trim away gristle, then season and brown until golden. Cheeks are naturally tough but the dense, lean meat becomes meltingly tender with slow, moist cooking, such as braising. They can also be marinated and stuffed before being cooked.

Heart

A fresh heart from a cow is bright red and firm. It is a naturally muscular organ, cheap to buy and flavourful when cooked. The older the animal, the tougher the heart and the longer it will require braising, stewing or slow-roasting to tenderise it. A tender heart from a younger animal can be sliced and fried or cut into cubes, threaded onto skewers and grilled.

Tripe

Tripe is the lining taken from one of the cow's four stomachs, though only that from the first three stomachs is used for culinary purposes. Tripe has a characteristic sponge-like or honeycomb appearance and texture. It is usually boiled in salted water or stock, then stewed or braised. It can then be marinated before being fried or grilled. Blanket tripe – also known as double tripe – is taken from the first, largest stomach and is smoother than tripe taken from the second and third stomachs.

Sweetbreads

Sweetbreads is the culinary name given both to the thymus gland in the throat and the pancreas in the stomach of the cow. Both types of sweetbreads are delicately flavoured and they can be prepared in the same way – by poaching briefly in water or a light stock. They can then be dusted with flour and fried until hot and creamy inside or they can be roasted or braised.

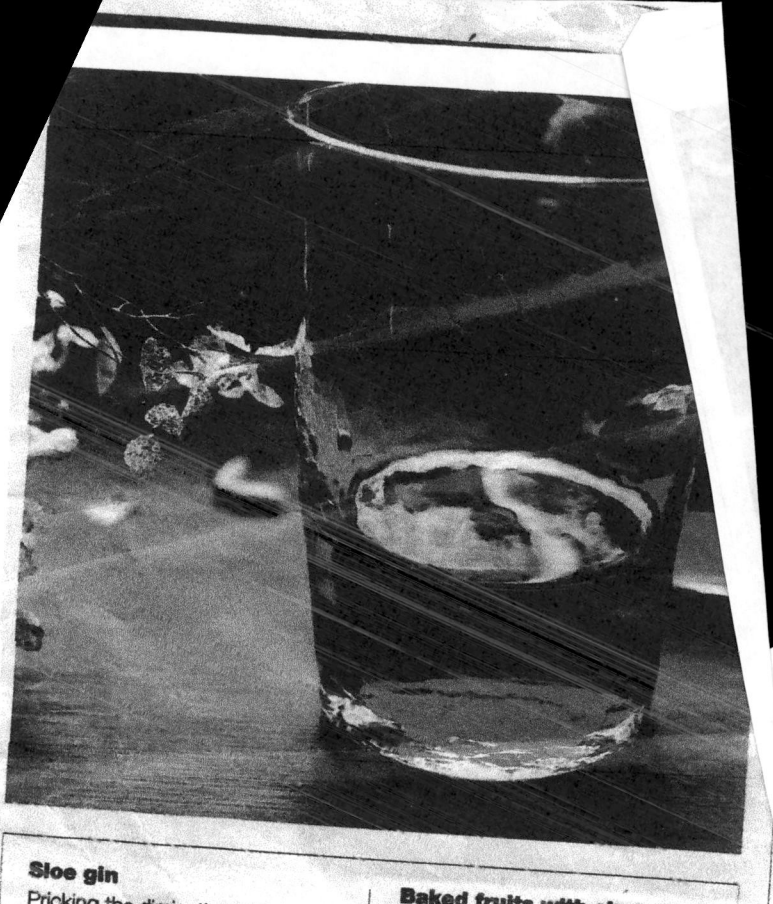

Sloe gin

Pricking the diminutive fruits with a needle is less fiddly than it sounds – a job to do on a damp Saturday afternoon. The jars, filled with sugar, gin and fruit, need turning regularly till the sugar has dissolved, then tucking away in ̤ corner for a couple of ̤ the magic gets to ̤ ems an ̤ open

Baked fruits with sloe gin

serves 4. The marriage of fruits and sloe gin produces a heady dessert with glowing, garnet juices. You don't need cream, and don't even think of custard. If you can't make your own sloe gin (sloes are not exacly something you can pick up at the supermarket), the website bramleyandgage.co.uk will send a bottle by post.

700g plums, rhubarb, apricots, damsons or peaches

̤ugar

̤in

̤k 4.

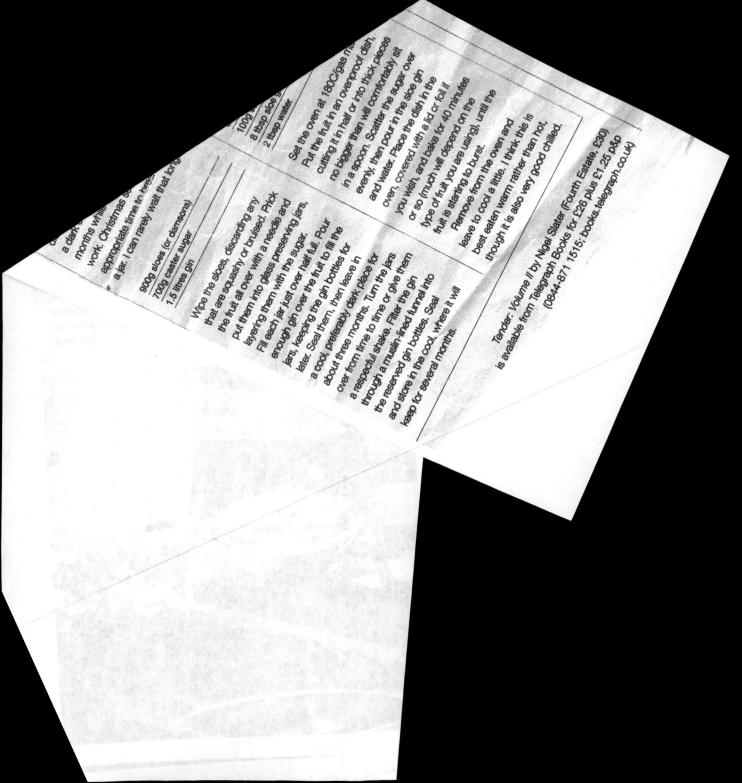

100g ...
8 tbsp sloe g...
2 tbsp water

a dark c...
months while...
work. Christmas s...
appropriate time to bre...
a jar. I can rarely wait that long...

900g sloes (or damsons)
700g caster sugar
1.5 litres gin

Wipe the sloes, discarding any that are squashy or bruised. Prick the fruit all over with a needle and put them into glass preserving jars, layering them with the sugar. Fill each jar just over half full. Pour enough gin over the fruit to fill the jars, keeping the gin bottles for later. Seal them, then leave in a cool, preferably dark place for about three months. Turn the jars over from time to time or give them a respectful shake. Filter the gin through a muslin-lined funnel into the reserved gin bottles. Seal and store in the cool, where it will keep for several months.

Set the oven at 180C/gas ma... Put the fruit in an ovenproof dish, cutting it in half or into thick pieces no bigger than will comfortably sit in a spoon. Scatter the sugar over evenly, then pour in the sloe gin and water. Place the dish in the oven, covered with a lid or foil if you wish, and bake for 40 minutes or so (much will depend on the type of fruit you are using), until the fruit is starting to burst.

Remove from the oven and leave to cool a little. I think this is best eaten warm rather than hot, though it is also very good chilled.

Tender: Volume II by Nigel Slater (Fourth Estate, £30) is available from Telegraph Books for £26 plus £1.25 p&p (0844-871 1515; books.telegraph.co.uk)

Liver

Cows' liver has a strong flavour
and is tougher and cheaper to
buy than calves' liver. Liver from
these older animals requires
braising or stewing to tenderise it.

Kidneys

To prepare kidneys, first remove
the central fatty core, the outer
membrane and any blood vessels,
then rinse in cold water. Cows'
kidneys can be relatively tough,
and require slow, moist cooking
such as braising or stewing.

Oxtail

Oxtail is the name given to the tail from any type of beef cattle. It is sold cut into pieces and, while meaty, it is also bony, and contains plenty of connective tissue that breaks down into a gelatineous liquid during slow cooking, such as braising. Oxtail soup is a richly flavoured dish.

Testicles

Bulls' testicles are known as fries and are served as a delicacy in certain parts of Europe. To prepare, blanch them in boiling water, refresh, then remove the skin. They can then be marinated and sliced into pieces, floured and fried, and are particularly tasty served with a lemon- or vinegar-based dressing and freshly chopped herbs.

Udder

The udder is the mammary gland of the cow and, although seldom used in cooking today, it was particularly popular in the Middle Ages. It can be sliced and soaked in cold water, before being blanched, then braised or roasted. Udder is a fatty meat that can also be finely minced and used in forcemeat (a smooth stuffing), pâtés and terrines.

Beef bones

Bones from the leg, knuckle or neck vertebrae are rich in connective
tissue and are useful for flavouring and adding texture to stocks, broths
and gravies. They are sometimes known as bouillon bones and can be
acquired cheaply from a butcher or can be taken from a cooked roast.
For a flavoursome beef stock, roast beef bones until golden. Add to a
pan of cold water with herbs and chopped vegetables and simmer into
a rich stock. Beef bones containing marrow will yield gelatinee, adding
extra flavour and texture. Bones are an excellent conductor of heat and
lend a great flavour to bone-in roasts.

Marrow

Bone marrow is the soft, fatty tissue found in the hollow cavities of
the leg and thigh bones of a cow carcass. It is cooked in the bone,
usually by poaching. A marrow bone added to a stock pot will lend a
gelatineous, silky texture and a deep flavour. Beef marrow can also be
served as a delicacy in the bone it was cooked in, with a teaspoon or
small scoop-like utensil to pick it from the bone before spreading it
onto bread or toast.

Veal

Veal is the meat from a calf slaughtered up to the age of 12 months. The production of veal is closely linked to the dairy industry. In order to produce milk, cows must produce calves. Female calves are raised for the dairy industry; males are slaughtered for their meat.

There are various methods of farming veal calves, each affecting the outcome of the meat. Some veal calves are removed from their mothers at birth, kept indoors, fed only milk and slaughtered before they are one month old. Meat from these calves is pale and tender. Others are allowed more freedom outdoors. They exist on a diet of hay and grain and are kept alive for longer. Meat from calves raised in this way is firmer textured and darker in colour.

While veal cuts can be incredibly tender, they have less fat and marbling than beef and often require slower cooking. When buying veal, choose cuts that are firm and dry without too much outside fat.

Shoulder and blade

The shoulder and blade primal of the veal carcass is cut from the
same area as the chuck primal of the beef animal. It includes the first
four ribs and the neck. The shoulder and blade is somewhat tougher
and less tender than the veal leg, though it has great flavour when
roasted or stewed. The veal shoulder can be cut into the point or flat
cut, comparable to the brisket primal of the beef animal. The point is
a smaller, fattier cut than the larger, leaner flat cut. Neck of veal is an
economical cut, yet tougher still than the shoulder; it is best suited to
stewing or grinding into hamburgers.

Veal shoulder arm roast

*This cut contains the arm bone
and rib bone. It is best suited
to braising or roasting.*

Veal shoulder
blade roast

*This cut contains the blade
bone, ribs and part of the
backbone. It is best suited to
braising or roasting or can
also be sliced into steaks for
braising, frying or grilling.*

Centre leg roast

This cut is incredibly tender. It can be bone-in or boned, then stuffed, rolled and roasted. Also known as leg centre cut and leg roast. Steaks can be cut from the centre leg roast. Feet are used for flavouring stocks and stews. They contain little meat and are rich in gelatinee, adding a delectable texture and richness to stews.

Veal shank

This is cut from the leg. It can be braised or pot-roasted whole or sliced through the bone for Italy's famous dish osso buco – 'osso' meaning bone and 'buco' hole. The marrow from the bone can be picked out with a toothpick or other small utensil.

Leg or round

The leg or round is sometimes known as hind-saddle of veal. The leg cut usually includes the sirloin (although the sirloin is sometimes included in the loin primal), the rump and the hind-shank. Cuts from the leg and round are great for roasting or braising – either boned or bone-in – and can be cut into cutlets or tender boneless slices. Leg cuts are also known as *escalope de veau* (French), sirloin chop, sirloin steak and *Schnitzel* (Germany and Austria). Roasts are also known as eye of round roast, rump roast, sirloin roast and top round roast.

Veal cutlets

These are taken from the centre of the top round and contain some of the marrow bone. Veal birds are cut from the eye of the cutlet. These tender cuts are pounded and rolled and are best suited to frying or grilling.

Scaloppine

This is a thin cut from the centre of the leg (or sometimes the loin). It should be cut to order, pounded flat then fried.

Sirloin of veal

This cut is often classed as part of the leg primal. It can be cut into roasts – a bone-in standing sirloin roast (also known as rump roast) and a boned rolled double sirloin roast (also known as double rump roast). The sirloin can also be cut into chops and steaks.

Breast and rib

The breast and rib primal contains the rack and ribs 6 to 12. The breast, taken from the underside of the rib, can contain the lower ribs or can be cut into a boneless roast. Although it has great flavour, it is a relatively tough, slightly fatty cut. It is best suited to slow, moist cooking such as braising or slow-roasting. Cuts from the breast are also known as flank and *poitrine de veau* (French).

Crown roast of veal

This is made by curving and tying the ribs together into a circle or crown shape. The crown is usually stuffed before being roasted and is often served as a splendid centrepiece at elegant celebrations.

Veal hotel rack

This contains the rib bones or can be boned into a veal rack rib-eye. It is succulent and flavoursome and can be cut into veal rack rib chops. If the meat is cut away to expose the bone, the chop is known as a Frenched rib chop.

Short ribs

These are taken from the rib roast and can be braised like beef short ribs.

Loin

The veal loin lies between the rib section and the sirloin (upper hip).
It is sold in two sections – the short and the butt – and also includes the
fillet. Cuts from the loin are expensive, tender and can be cut into small
bone-in or boneless roasts, chops, steaks and cutlets. The kidneys and
sirloin are sometimes included in the loin primal (although the sirloin
can also be included in the leg primal). Thin, boneless slices known as
scaloppine can be cut from the loin.

Loin roast of veal

*This contains the T-shaped
bones and can be cut into
T-bone chops, which include
part of the eye and the
fillet. These are best grilled
or roasted.*

Loin roast

*This is a bone-in roast. If the
bones are removed, it is known
as a rolled loin roast and can
be stuffed, rolled and tied.*

Veal fillet

*This cut lies beneath the
ribs. It is a tender cut for
roasting or can be sliced
into medallions for veal
saltimbocca, a dish that
involves wrapping medallions
of veal with prosciutto, sage
and lemon and frying in
butter and wine. Fillet is also
known as tenderloin, veal
tender and filet (French).*

Loin veal chops

*These are similar to loin
chops but traditionally
include a slice of kidney, often
skewered in place. They are
best suited to roasting
or grilling.*

Veal offal

Offal from the veal calf is incredibly tender and is more highly valued than the organ meats of all other animals.

Veal brains

These are creamy and delicately flavoured. They are a particularly popular delicacy in Europe.

Veal cheeks

These come from the cheek part of the calf's head and are similar to beef cheeks. They are best suited to braising and slow-roasting.

Veal kidneys

These should be plump and mild-smelling. They are more delicately flavoured than beef kidneys and are naturally tender. They can be fried or grilled whole or sliced, until just pink inside (they can become a little tough if overcooked).

Veal head

This can be cooked and presented in numerous and elaborate ways. Also known as tête de veau *(French), it is usually poached or braised and sliced into broths or used in terrines and pies.*

Veal sweetbreads

These are similar in texture to veal brains. As with beef, sweetbreads is the culinary name given to the thymus gland in the throat and the pancreas in the stomach of the veal calf. Delicately flavoured, veal sweetbreads are an expensive choice but are delicious poached, then dusted in flour and fried in butter.

Veal tongue

This is smaller and less tough than beef tongue. It is best braised or poached.

Calves' liver

This is pale pink and mildly flavoured compared with liver from other animals. It has an incredibly smooth texture and can vary in appearance, from pale to dark in colour, depending on how the animal was reared. It can be fried in butter, grilled until tender or wrapped in bacon and roasted.

Beef products

Salt beef

Salt beef is made by curing brisket or flank. Sometimes chuck, or the leaner cut silverside (from the bottom round), is used. In the US it is called corned beef. The 'corn' refers to the grains of salt used in the brine in which the meat is cured, before being poached in water. It can then be pot-roasted and is traditionally served with mustard, vegetables and boiled potatoes. Leftovers can be thinly sliced and served cold in rye bread sandwiches with mustard and pickles.

Dried and smoked beef

Jerky originated in South Africa. It is made by salting and air-drying a variety of meat, such as beef or game. Jerky is almost black in colour, can be stored at room temperature and is tough and chewy to eat. It is also known as jerked beef or biltong.

Bresaola is an Italian delicacy made from cuts of beef taken from the round that are cured with salt, then air-dried. It is cut into wafer-thin slices and should be moist and delicately flavoured.

Pastrami is made from smoked corned beef. It is often served cold in sandwiches, though can also be served hot with vegetables and potatoes.

Suet

Suet is the hard white fat taken from a cow's kidneys. It was
traditionally used for frying as it has a high smoking point;
fish and chips in Great Britain were fried in suet until healthier oils
became more popular. Suet is the fat used in suet pastry and in sweet
and savoury dumplings and puddings, including Christmas pudding
and mincemeat. It is usually sold shredded – often dusted in flour to
keep it from clumping together – or in blocks which need to be grated
before being added to other ingredients.

Sausage

Sausages can be fresh, cured, dried, smoked or pre-cooked. There are numerous varieties; in Germany alone there are hundreds. Sausages can be made from any type of chopped or minced meat, which is often combined with fat, variety meats and other fillers – depending on the quality of the sausage – then seasoned with herbs and spices. The mix is pushed into tubular casings, traditionally made from animal intestines, although now usually synthetic. Fresh sausages can be fried, grilled, roasted or cooked in a stew or braise. A good quality fresh sausage is firm, meaty and well seasoned. Cured sausage, such as Italian or German salami, Spanish chorizo and French saucisson, can be made from beef. These do not need to be cooked and can be eaten cold. Black sausages – also known as black pudding – are made from blood and diced fat.

Techniques

How to fry a steak

A steak can be cooked from rare to well done. Timing is everything and knowing how to cook a steak just as you like it is a useful skill to master. Piercing a steak with a meat thermometer is not advisable because it will let out all the lovely juices; neither is cutting into it to check before it is served, because it will spoil the presentation. The cooking time depends on the thickness of the steak, rather than its weight. Other factors such as the temperature and heat distribution of the pan and the temperature of the steak before it was added to the pan play a part too.

Recommended cooking times for frying a ¾-inch-
thick sirloin steak from room temperature in a
preheated pan are as follows:

Rare	1½ minutes per side
Medium-rare	2 minutes per side
Medium	2½ minutes per side
Well done	3½ minutes per side

Rare

Medium

Medium well done

Well done

The cheek, chin and forehead test

An accurate way to test for doneness is to press the steak lightly with your fingertip and compare the way it feels to your cheek, chin and forehead. A rare steak is soft and fleshy like your cheek; fleshy with some resistance, like your chin, is medium; firmer to the touch with more resistance, like your forehead, means it is well done.

The thumb test

Relax one hand and touch the fleshy part at the base of your thumb with your other index finger. It will feel soft and fleshy, like raw meat. Press the tip of your thumb against the tip of your forefinger on the same hand. Now feel the base of the thumb again. It will feel slightly tighter; this is like rare meat. Move your thumb from the forefinger to the middle finger, and the pad at the base of the thumb will feel a little tighter still; this is medium meat. Press your thumb against the tip of your fourth finger and it will tighten more; this is medium-to-well-done. Stretch the thumb to the little finger and the muscles in the base of the thumb will be tight and contracted, which is how well-done meat feels.

Meatballs

Meatballs can be made from minced beef, lamb or
pork, which is seasoned with salt and pepper and
shaped into small balls. Freshly chopped herbs,
such as parsley and rosemary, and diced onion can
be added for extra flavour. Sometimes breadcrumbs
and beaten egg are added to bind the mixture
together, though this is not strictly necessary, acting
rather as a bulking agent and ultimately lessening
the flavour and texture of the meatballs.

Using clean, wet hands, shape the seasoned minced
meat into small balls (wetting your hands first will
keep the meat from sticking to your fingers). Brown
the meatballs in a large frying pan until golden all
over – this browning will enhance the final flavour
of the dish. When sufficiently golden, add tinned
tomatoes or a tomato-based sauce, then cover and
cook for at least 20 minutes until the meat is tender
and cooked through. You can remove the lid for
the last 10 minutes of cooking time to allow the
sauce to reduce and thicken. Sprinkle with freshly
chopped herbs and some grated cheese and serve
with spaghetti.

Suet pastry

Suet – hard white beef fat – is most commonly used to make pastry. Suet pastry is made by mixing self-raising flour and half the amount of suet with just enough iced water to bind the mixture together to form a dough. If the suet is fresh, it should be chilled and grated into the dry ingredients and blended into the flour with fingertips. Adding too much water or overworking the dough will result in a tough pastry. The dough is then rolled out on a floured surface and used to line a buttered pudding basin. This can then be filled and topped with a suet pastry lid. To cook, the pudding is covered with waxed paper and foil, set into a pan of simmering water and steamed until the filling is cooked through.

Carpaccio

Carpaccio is a classic dish that originated in Venice. Very fresh, raw beef fillet is placed in the freezer until just firm. It is then very thinly sliced, arranged on a plate and dressed. There are many variations of the dressing but it often includes mayonnaise, vinegar, lemon juice and sometimes mustard. The beef can also be topped with chopped onions and capers. Sometimes a simple dressing of olive oil and balsamic vinegar is used and the dish is sprinkled with Parmesan cheese. Carpaccio is typically served as an appetiser rather than a main course and today the term carpaccio can also refer to very thinly sliced raw vegetables and fish.

Steak tartare

Steak tartare is a classic dish made from very fresh, finely chopped raw beef fillet seasoned with a combination of olive oil, lemon juice, French mustard, finely chopped onion, parsley, capers, gherkins and plenty of salt and pepper. The mixture is pressed into a ring on the plate and topped with a raw egg or egg yolk (alternatively the raw egg can be stirred into the mixture). Sometimes the dish is assembled at the table by the waiter, and it is traditionally served with crisp French fries.

Chilli-braised beef, New Mexican-style

Pieces of chuck, chillies and peppers are braised together until tender in this New Mexican pot-roast. Enjoy shreds of the meat and peppers wrapped up in soft flour tortillas, with diced avocado, salsa and sour cream on the side.

Serves 4–6

4–5 mild dried chillies
1 green pepper, deseeded
and sliced
1 red pepper, deseeded
and sliced
4 ripe tomatoes, diced
1 small to medium bunch
coriander, chopped
5 garlic cloves, chopped
1 onion, chopped
2 fresh bay leaves
1½ tsp ground cumin
1–1½kg (2–3lb) chuck steak
or chuck pot-roast, cut into
2.5cm (1in) cubes
250ml (8fl oz) beef stock
250ml (8fl oz) ale

Lightly toast the chillies over an open flame, then put them in a bowl. Cover with hot water and soak for at least 1 hour.

Preheat the oven to 175°C (350°F/Gas mark 4).

Discard the stems, skin and seeds of the chillies and put half the flesh into a baking tin with half the peppers, tomatoes, coriander, garlic, onion, bay leaves and cumin. Top with the meat, then layer over the remaining half of the ingredients. Season with salt, add the stock and ale, then cover tightly with foil.

Bake for 2 to 3 hours, adding more liquid if necessary, or until the meat is tender. Remove the foil and bake for 30 minutes more, increasing the heat if necessary to brown and crisp the top. Serve hot.

Italial braised beef with onion and aubergine

This is the perfect prepare-ahead dinner or supper party dish, using beef shanks. It is perfect served with this simple vegetable stir-fry.

Serves 4

Preheat the oven to 160°C (325°F/Gas mark 3).

Mix together the flour and chilli powder on a large plate. Add the shanks and turn to coat them in the flour mixture.

Heat 3 tbsp olive oil in a large flameproof, ovenproof dish. Add the floured shanks and brown well all over. Stir in the sliced garlic, oregano, tomatoes and just enough stock to cover the meat. Bring to the boil, then cover and transfer to the oven. Bake for 3 hours or until the shanks are meltingly tender.

Heat the remaining oil in a hot frying pan. Add the aubergine and fry until golden. Add the onion and fry for 3 minutes, then add the pepper and chopped garlic and stir-fry for 2 minutes.

Remove the shanks from the sauce, transfer to a plate, cover with foil and keep warm. Add the stir-fried vegetables to the sauce and simmer, uncovered, for 5 to 10 minutes until the vegetables are tender and the sauce is well reduced.

Meanwhile, dry-fry the pancetta in the pan until crisp.

To serve, divide the vegetables and sauce between four plates and top each with a shank. Spoon over the remaining sauce, then garnish with the pancetta and some chopped parsley.

2 tbsp plain flour
1 tsp mild chilli powder
4 beef shanks, each weighing
about 175g (6oz), trimmed
5 tbsp olive oil
2 large garlic cloves, sliced,
and 1 garlic clove,
finely chopped
2 tbsp chopped fresh oregano
400g tin chopped tomatoes
500ml (16fl oz) beef or
vegetable stock
2 medium aubergines, cut
into 5cm (2in) chunks
1 large onion, cut into sixths
1 red onion, cut into sixths
1 red pepper, deseeded
and diced
8 slices pancetta or very
thin bacon
Chopped parsley, to garnish

Old-fashioned pot-roast with onion gravy

There are many recipes for pot-roast – all of which involve browning a large cut of beef, then adding a splash of liquid to the pot and cooking it slowly. This delightfully old-fashioned recipe uses tomato juice to moisten the meat, keeping it tender and making a flavoursome gravy.

Serves 8–10

*2.25–2.75kg (5–6lb)
brisket, trimmed
1 tbsp plain flour
4 tbsp vegetable oil
6 onions, cut into
½-inch rings
4–6 garlic cloves,
finely chopped
250ml (8fl oz) tomato juice
½ tsp dried thyme
½ tsp paprika
1 bay leaf
6 carrots, cut into ¼-inch
slices on the diagonal
Parsley sprigs, to garnish*

Rinse the brisket under cold running water and pat dry with paper towels. Put onto a plate and dust with flour. Heat 2 tbsp oil in a large flameproof, ovenproof dish. Add the brisket and cook for 5 to 7 minutes until browned on the underside. Turn and cook for 5 to 6 minutes until browned. Transfer to a plate.

Preheat the oven to 325°F (170°C).

Add the remaining oil to the dish. Stir in the onions and cook until softened. Add the garlic and cook for 1 minute, then add the tomato juice, scraping any bits from the bottom of the dish. Add the thyme, paprika and bay leaf and season with salt and pepper.

Return the brisket to the dish with enough water to cover all the ingredients. Bring to a boil, skimming off any foam from the surface. Cover tightly and bake in the oven for 3 hours or until the brisket is tender. Add the carrots and cook for 30 minutes more, or until tender.

If the sauce is quite thin, remove the brisket to a deep serving platter to keep warm. Put the dish on the hob and bubble until the sauce is reduced and thickened. Carve the brisket into ¼-inch slices, then divide between four plates. Spoon over the sauce and garnish with parsley.

Braised beef with white radish

Cooking this Korean casserole slowly will result in a rich, thick sauce that will coat the ribs and radish. The tasty ribs will add lots of flavour to the dish.

Serves 4

Make a few deep slashes in a lattice pattern on the meaty side of each rib, then add to a large saucepan of boiling water. Return to the boil, simmer for 1 minute, then drain and rinse the ribs under cold water.

Put the ribs and white radish in a large skillet with 500ml (16fl oz) water and bring to the boil. Cover and simmer gently for 40 minutes.

Meanwhile, soak the Chinese mushrooms in hot water for 20 minutes. Remove with a slotted spoon and cut away any hard parts, including the stems.

Add the garlic, soy sauce, toasted sesame oil and seeds, sugar and plenty of freshly ground black pepper to the ribs. Return to the boil, then lower the heat and cook, partly covered, for 20 minutes.

Add the mushrooms and cook, stirring occasionally, for 30 minutes or until the ribs are tender. Remove the lid, raise the heat and bubble until the sauce is reduced to a few spoonfuls. Serve with rice and steamed green vegetables.

1.4kg (3lb) beef back ribs, cut into 5cm (2in) segments
450g (1lb) white radish, cut into 5cm (2in) cubes
8 dried Chinese black mushrooms
4–6 garlic cloves, crushed
5 tbsp soy sauce
1 tbsp toasted sesame oil
2 tbsp toasted sesame seeds
2 tbsp light brown sugar

Hanger steak

This steak, also called hanging tender or bistro steak, can sometimes be hard to find, so ask your butcher to order it in. The dark meat is exceptionally juicy and has a sublime flavour.

Serves 4

4 hanger steaks
Olive oil, for brushing
Lemon zest, to garnish

Preheat the grill or barbecue.

Remove all fat and sinew from the steaks, rinse and pat dry with paper towels. Remove the centre sheet of gristle from each steak and cut each into two pieces.

Brush the steaks with oil, and season. Cook under the grill or on the barbecue, turning frequently, so they cook evenly all over – this will take about 4–5 minutes under a grill, or 10 minutes on the barbecue. Take care not to cook beyond medium or they will become tough.

Carve into slices against the grain, sprinkle with the lemon zest and serve with potatoes and a salad.

Cuban beef with peppers and spices

This hearty Cuban dish is known as *vaca frita*. Flank steak is full of flavour, and the leftovers are great in sandwiches with mayonnaise and mustard. The cooking liquid can be strained and reserved for soup.
Serves 6

Put the flank steak in a pot with one-third of the onion, the carrot, one-third of the garlic, the stock cubes and enough water to cover. Bring to the boil, then simmer over a very low heat, adding more water to keep the meat covered. Cook for 1½ to 2 hours, then leave to cool in the liquid.

Remove the beef from the liquid. Shred it into a bowl, season with salt and pepper then toss with two-thirds of the lime juice, the cumin seeds, chilli powder and oregano.

Heat 1–2 tbsp olive oil in a heavy non-stick frying pan. Add about half of the remaining onion and fry until soft. Season with salt and set aside. Fry the peppers in a little oil until softened, then set aside.

To make the salsa, put the remaining garlic into a bowl and mix in the remaining onion and lime juice, the tomatoes, coriander and green chilli. Set aside.

Heat 1–2 tbsp olive oil in the frying pan. Add the meat mixture in batches and sauté for 5 minutes over a high heat until browned. Repeat until all the meat is crisp and browned. Return the fried onions and peppers to the pan, mix well and serve with the salsa, lime wedges, sour cream and spring onions.

1kg (2lb) flank steak
3 onions, thinly sliced
1 carrot, chopped
6–8 garlic cloves, chopped
1–2 beef stock cubes
50–100ml (2–4fl oz) lime juice
½ tsp cumin seeds
½ tsp mild chilli powder
½ tsp dried oregano
50ml (2 fl oz) extra-virgin
olive oil
1 green pepper, deseeded
and chopped
1 red pepper, deseeded
and chopped
2 ripe tomatoes, diced
5 tbsp chopped coriander
1–2 fresh green
chillies, chopped
Wedges of lime, sour cream
and thinly sliced spring
onions, to serve

Prosciutto tournedos

Wrapping prosciutto around the steak gives the meat a wonderful Italian flavour. This dish is best served with a glass of Chianti. Cuts from the fillet are particularly tender and require little in the way of cooking or preparation.

Serves 4

250g (½lb) spinach
¼ tsp grated nutmeg
50g (2oz) ricotta cheese
4 slices bread
A little butter or olive oil,
for frying
4 slices prosciutto
4 fillet steaks
or medallions, each
weighing 100g (4oz)
2 tomatoes, halved

Bring a pan of water to the boil and cook the spinach for 2 minutes. Drain, pressing out any excess water, then mix with the nutmeg and ricotta. Season with salt and pepper.

Cut out a round of bread from each slice, discarding the crusts, then fry on both sides in the butter or olive oil until golden. Transfer to a serving plate and spoon the spinach mixture on top. Set aside in a warm place.

Cut the prosciutto into strips the same width as the steaks. Wind the strips firmly around the steaks, season then grill or fry until golden. Serve on top of the spinach mixture and top each with half a tomato.

Steak bordelaise

For the best texture and flavour choose well-marbled sirloin steaks. The bordelaise sauce can be made with red or white wine – go for whichever you're drinking.

Serves 4

To make the sauce, put the shallot into a small pan with 4 tbsp butter and 2 tbsp water and simmer until the water has evaporated and the shallot starts to fry – take care that it does not brown.

Add the wine, bring to the boil and reduce by at least two-thirds. Add the stock and the remaining butter, then bring to the boil. Simmer until thickened, then add the parsley. Mix well, season to taste and set aside.

Heat a large frying pan until very hot. Add the steaks – in batches if necessary – and cook to your preference. Remove from the pan and keep warm. Add the sauce to the pan, stirring into the pan juices and bubble for 1 minute until hot.

Divide the steaks between four plates, spoon over the sauce and garnish with parsley.

4 tbsp finely chopped shallot
6 tbsp unsalted butter
125ml (4fl oz) red or white wine
125ml (4fl oz) beef stock
2 tbsp chopped parsley, plus extra to garnish
4 225g (8oz) sirloin steaks

Warm shredded beef salad

This slightly sweet dressing, together with the caramelized strips of beef, make a mouthwatering salad.
Serves 4

3 tbsp soy sauce
1 tbsp sweet sherry
½ tsp ground mixed
peppercorns
¼ tsp chilli powder
1 tsp honey
700g (1½lb) sirloin steaks,
trimmed and cut into
thin strips
A handful of mixed
salad leaves
1 tbsp mirin
1 tbsp peanut oil, plus 2 tsp
1 tsp rice wine vinegar
1 tsp toasted sesame oil
2 tsp cornflour, sieved
¼ tsp salt
4 spring onions, sliced on
the diagonal
Sesame seeds, to garnish

To make the marinade, mix together the soy sauce, sherry, ground peppercorns, chilli powder and honey in a shallow dish. Add the beef and turn to coat. Marinate for 30 minutes.

Put the salad leaves in a bowl. Mix together the mirin, 1 tbsp peanut oil and the rice wine vinegar, then drizzle over the leaves.

Drain the beef and pat dry on paper towels. Add the toasted sesame oil and 2 tsp peanut oil to a wok or large frying pan. Sprinkle the cornflour and salt over the beef, then immediately add to the hot pan. Stir-fry over a high heat until crisp, then spoon onto the salad.

Mix well, sprinkle with the spring onions and serve warm, garnished with sesame seeds.

Beef Stroganoff

Beef knuckle gives this dish a wonderful, rich flavour, and simmering the mushrooms in the wine adds a delightful piquancy. Plain noodles are the best accompaniment.

Serves 4

700g (1½lb) beef knuckle, cut into 1cm (½in) slices
6 tbsp butter
1 medium onion, chopped
350g (12oz) mushrooms, sliced
2 tsp paprika
2 pinches of ground nutmeg
4 tbsp white wine
250ml (8fl oz) sour cream

Put the beef slices between two sheets of non-stick baking parchment and beat with a meat tenderiser to thin them out. Slice into 2.5cm- (1in-) wide strips.

Melt the butter in a large, heavy frying pan. Quickly sauté the beef, turning it regularly to brown it lightly all over. Season, then remove with a slotted spoon and set aside.

Add the onion to the buttery juices in the pan and cook, stirring, until soft. Add the mushrooms and cook for 5 to 10 minutes until golden. Add the paprika, nutmeg and wine, bring to the boil, then simmer until the liquid has reduced to one-quarter of the original amount.

Add the sour cream and simmer to a thick coating consistency. Return the meat to the pan and return to a simmer. Serve with noodles.

Steak au poivre

This is just one version of this timelessly popular dish. Marinating the steak enables the pepper flavour to penetrate the meat, while the cream cools its heat.

Serves 4

Sprinkle 2 tsp pepper and the garlic over one side of the steaks and press well in. Leave for 30 minutes.

Brush a ridged griddle pan with oil and heat until almost smoking. Add the steaks – in batches if necessary – peppered-side down, and cook to your preference, turning once. Remove the steaks from the pan and set aside to keep warm.

Meanwhile, put the brandy, butter and remaining pepper into a large frying pan. Heat to melt the butter and reduce the liquid to 1 tbsp. Add the cream, crème fraîche and beef glaze or stock, if using. Bring to a simmer, then reduce to a light coating consistency.

3 tsp ground black pepper
2 garlic cloves, crushed
4 225g (8oz) top round
(rump)steaks
a little oil, for brushing
125ml (4fl oz) brandy
2 tbsp butter
250ml (8fl oz) single cream
125ml (4fl oz) crème fraîche or
sour cream
1 tsp beef glaze or
stock (optional)

Add the steaks, peppered-side up, to the skillet. Bubble for 20 seconds, then divide the steaks between four plates and spoon over the sauce. Serve with potatoes and vegetables.

Grilled veal kebabs

This recipe originates from the Portuguese island of Madeira, where it is known as *espetada*. It is a great way to tenderise and add flavour to veal. Choose a cut of veal from the loin or leg.

Serves 4

Thread the veal onto four skewers and lay flat in a shallow, non-metallic dish. Mix together the garlic, bay leaf, herbs, wine and oil and season with black pepper. Drizzle over the veal, turning to coat, then leave in a cool place for 2 hours, turning occasionally.

Preheat the grill. Remove the veal from the marinade and pat dry on paper towels. Brush lightly with oil and grill, turning occasionally, until just cooked through. Sprinkle with salt and serve.

575–750g (1¼–1½lb) veal,
cut into 2.5cm (1in) cubes
1–2 plump garlic
cloves, crushed
1 bay leaf, torn in half
a small handful of parsley
mixed with a little fresh
marjoram, chopped
6 tbsp red or dry white wine
2 tbsp olive oil, plus extra
for brushing

Veal with onion and tuna sauce

This classic Italian dish, known as *vitello tonnato*, makes an elegant summer supper. It is the perfect prepare-ahead meal for relaxed entertaining. Choose a cut from the leg, which is ideal for braising.
Serves 6–8

1kg (2¼lb) boneless veal roast, trimmed
12 anchovy fillets, chopped
3 onions, finely chopped
2 tbsp capers, roughly chopped
6 black peppercorns
4 large parsley sprigs
500ml (16fl oz) chicken or vegetable stock
100g (3½oz) tinned tuna, drained
1 shallot, finely chopped
1 tbsp tomato purée
Juice of 1 lemon
250ml (8fl oz) mayonnaise
2 tbsp chopped flat-leaf parsley

Put the veal onto a cutting board and butterfly it, slicing it open – without cutting completely through – into one large, evenly thick piece. Pound half the anchovies, one of the chopped onions, the capers and a little black pepper together into a chunky paste, then rub over the veal. Roll up the veal, tie it securely then place in a pan just large enough to hold it.

Press the remaining chopped onions, peppercorns and parsley around the veal, then pour in just enough stock to cover it. Bring to the boil, then half-cover and simmer gently for 2 hours, until the veal is just tender. Leave to cool in the stock, then chill (ideally overnight).

To make the tuna sauce, purée the tuna in a blender with the shallot, remaining anchovies, tomato purée, lemon juice and mayonnaise. Season with black pepper and stir in the parsley. Slice the veal, arrange on a plate and spoon over the sauce.

Spiced oxtails with buckwheat

This recipe, adapted from one popular in the Lower Volga region of Russia, requires long, slow cooking but the meltingly tender results are well worth it.

Serves 6–8

In a large pan, brown the oxtail pieces in the oil. Remove with a slotted spoon and set aside. Add the onion and fry until softened. Stir in the garlic and cook for 1 minute, then stir in the tomato purée, tomatoes, stock, cinnamon, cumin, ginger, mustard seeds, turmeric, parsley and coriander. Return the meat to the pan. Bring to the boil, cover and simmer gently for 4 hours, topping up with water if necessary, until the meat is falling from the bone. Cool, then chill for 12 hours or overnight. Preheat the oven to 175°C (350°F/Gas mark 4). Toast the buckwheat in an ovenproof pan over a medium heat until it begins to pop. Add 500ml (20 fl oz) boiling water, a pinch of salt and the butter. Bake in the oven for 45 minutes or until the grains are soft. Meanwhile, discard the solidified fat from the oxtail dish. Remove the oxtail pieces and transfer to a baking dish. Pour over enough boiling water to cover the base of the dish, cover with foil and reheat in the oven for 30 minutes. Strain the tomato sauce mixture. Tip back into the pan with the carrots, turnips and celeriac. Bring to the boil, cover and simmer for 10 minutes. Stir in the courgette and leeks and cook until the vegetables are tender, about 10 minutes. Strain the oxtail and add the cooking liquid to the vegetable mixture. Bring the sauce to a boil. Spoon the buckwheat onto a large serving plate with the oxtails and vegetable mixture. Garnish with sprigs of parsley and coriander.

2.25kg (5lb) oxtail, trimmed
4 tbsp sunflower oil
3 medium onions, sliced
4 garlic cloves, crushed
1½ tbsp tomato purée
400g tin chopped tomatoes
with chilli
1l (30fl oz) beef stock
3 cinnamon sticks
1 tsp ground cumin
1 tsp ground ginger
1 tsp mustard seeds
¾ tsp turmeric
4 tbsp each finely chopped
parsley and coriander, plus
extra to garnish
350g (12oz) buckwheat groats
(kasha)
2 tbsp butter
3 carrots, halved and
thinly sliced
350g (12oz) turnips, halved
and thinly sliced
1 small celeriac, quartered
and thinly sliced
2 medium courgettes, halved
and thinly sliced
700g (½lb) baby leeks,
trimmed and left whole

PORK

Pork is the name of the meat taken
from the pig animal or carcass.
Almost all parts of the animal can
be eaten and the meat can be sold
fresh, pre-cooked, cured, marinated
or smoked. Pork is generally lean
and tender and its flavour goes with
various herbs, aromatic seasonings
and fruit, such as apples and
peaches. Pork is a versatile meat
and can be roasted, grilled, fried,
stewed, braised or poached. Fresh
pork should be moist and pink;
avoid cuts that are grey or red.

Primal cuts

The primal cuts are those made in the initial stage of butchering. They may be sold whole, or subdivided into smaller cuts for sale to home cooks.

Arm shoulder

Whole shoulder

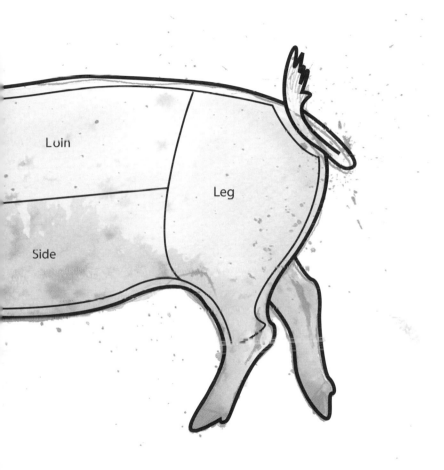

Loin

Leg

Side

Whole shoulder

The shoulder primal can be divided into two sub-cuts for roasts, braises and pork chops: the blade shoulder in the upper section and the spare rib chops taken from underneath. Chops cut from the shoulder are tougher than loin chops. The economical blade roast can be bone-in or boneless.

Flavour

The blade shoulder is relatively lean with great flavour, though it can be quite tough. Rectangular-shaped spare rib chops from the shoulder are particularly succulent and flavourful because of the fat running through them.

Cooking

Blade roast is best suited to roasting or slow cooking in moist heat, such as braising. It can also be cubed for stewing or minced for burgers and sausages. Spare rib pork chops are best suited to braising, grilling and barbecuing.

Also known as

Blade pork chops, shoulder butt, upper shoulder or Boston shoulder, chuck. Economical cuts from the blade are also known as grillades (French) and are used in the Louisiana dish grillades and grits.

Substitutes

Loin roast or loin chop.

Arm shoulder

*The arm shoulder primal is taken from beneath the blade
shoulder and includes the top of the foreleg. It can be cut
into roasts or steaks for braising or stewing. It is ideal for
using in sausages and in processed food.*

Flavour

*The arm shoulder is a tougher
cut than the blade shoulder.
It is lean and therefore not
particularly flavourful.*

Cooking

*Roasts or steaks can be braised
or stewed. Cuts from the arm
shoulder can also be minced
for burgers.*

Also known as

Hand of pork.

Flavour

The picnic shoulder is moderately flavourful. It can be smoked for extra flavour.

Picnic shoulder

The picnic shoulder is cut from the arm shoulder primal at the thick end of the belly (side). It can be either bone-in or boned and can be cut into steaks. The arm picnic roast contains the arm, shank and cushion. If the shank is removed it is known as pork shoulder arm roast. It can be subdivided into a smaller cut called the picnic cushion and into arm steaks.

Cooking

Roasts are best suited to roasting or slow cooking in moist heat, such as braising. The picnic shoulder can be roasted, braised or poached. It can be barbecued and is delicious as pulled pork. It is sliced and eaten cold for picnics. Steaks are best suited to grilling, frying or braising.

Also known as

Arm picnic roast.

Hock

Hock is the lower portion of the foreleg, beneath the shank.
It is an economical cut containing the shank bone and usually the skin.
Hock contains a lot of connective tissue and is relatively tough unless
cooked slowly.

Flavour

*It is naturally flavourful but
often smoked for extra flavour.*

Cooking

*Hock is best cooked slowly in
moist heat, such as braising
or stewing, to break down the
connective tissue. It gives out
a thick jelly when cooked and
is therefore used to add
richness and flavour to stocks,
stews and braises.*

Also known as

*Knuckle of bacon
(when smoked).*

Loin

The loin primal consists of the pig animal's back between the shoulder and the hind leg. The loin can be cut into roasts and chops.

Canadian-style bacon is cut from the loin. The chump end is a continuation of the loin; it runs towards the hind leg and can be cut into roasts or steaks.

Flavour
Cuts from the loin are lean and tender.

Cooking
Loin cuts generally cook quickly and are best suited to roasting or grilling. The chump end is best suited to roasting.

Flavour

Juicy, tender and flavourful.

Cooking

Best suited to roasting and grilling.

Hind loin

This is a more expensive cut from the centre of the loin. It consists of the tenderloin, loin eye and T-bones and makes an impressive roast to serve at the table. It can also be cut into pork chops.

Also known as

Centre loin and sirloin end roast. Hind loin chops are also known as bistecca *(Italian).*

Flavour

Tender, juicy, and flavourful.

Cooking

Loin roasts are best suited to roasting and grilling. Chops are best suited to grilling or frying. Cutlets can be fried, grilled or sliced into strips and stir-fried.

Also known as

Fore loin, rib loin, sirloin roast (bone in) and carré de porc *(French). Two racks of ribs curved and tied together is known as a crown roast.*

Rack of pork

The rack is cut from the rib end of the loin and consists of the rib bones, hip bone, backbone and loin eye muscle; it can include the larger end of the tenderloin. It can be cut into chops or cutlets. It can be bone-in or boned and rolled. If the chine bone (backbone) has been removed, it is known as having been chined. If the fat has been removed to expose the rib bones, it is described as Frenched.

Loin chops

Loin chops cut from the rack are a relatively expensive choice.
They contain the T-bone and a section of the loin and tenderloin.
Traditionally the chop included a slice of the kidney, though this is now
rare. They can be bone-in or boneless depending on whether the chine
bone has been removed. Boneless loin chops can be butterflied open by
being sliced almost in half and flattened out.

Top loin roast

The top loin roast is a boneless cut and contains the loin eye muscle.
Two top loin roasts can be tied together, fat side out, to become a loin
double roast.

Ribs

Pork ribs, cut from the rib section within the loin, consist ofthe bones and meat between them. They are best suited to slow, moist cooking, such as braising, but can also be grilled.

Country-style ribs

Cut from the fore or rib end of the loin, these popular ribs are small and meaty. They come in slabs of 8 to 14 ribs and can be a relatively pricey choice. They are shorter and meatier than spare ribs from the belly and take well to being marinated or seasoned by a rub before being braised. Also known as loin ribs, back ribs and baby-back ribs.

Flat bone riblets

These are small and flat in shape. Also known as button ribs.

Tenderloin

This is a long, boneless, wedge-shaped piece from the loin that runs alongside the backbone. The thin end towards the rack can be cut into smaller pieces.

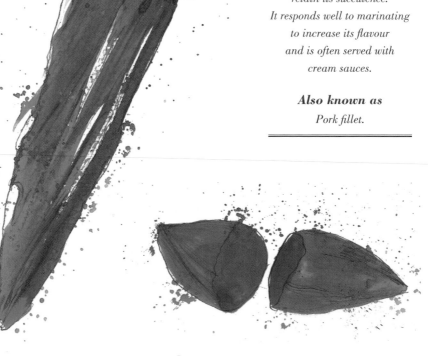

Flavour

The tenderloin is incredibly tender. It is not particularly flavourful because it is so lean.

Cooking

*Best suited to fast cooking, such as roasting or grilling. Take care not to overcook tenderloin because it can dry out easily. For this reason it is often stuffed and rolled to retain its succulence.
It responds well to marinating to increase its flavour and is often served with cream sauces.*

Also known as

Pork fillet.

Side

The side primal is cut from the underside of the pig carcass between the fore and hind legs. It consists of the pork belly and spare ribs. Pork brisket bones and rib tips can also be cut from the side. Cuts from the side can be cured and turned into bacon.

Flavour

The side has a good flavour due to its high fat content.

Cooking

Cuts from the side are best suited to slow roasting, braising and stewing. Bacon can be grilled or fried.

Pork belly

Pork belly is fatty, tough and relatively cheap. It can be sold boned,
stuffed or rolled.

Flavour

*Pork belly has an extremely
good flavour due to its high
ratio of fat to meat.*

Cooking

*Pork belly is suitable for
a variety of moist cooking
methods, including slow-
roasting, braising, stewing
and barbecuing. Pieces can
be cut into strips and grilled.
Pork belly responds well to
marinating – particularly
using Asian flavours – and
can also be prepared as a
confit or terrine or shredded
into rillettes.*

Also known as

Pork side or trimmed belly.

Spare ribs

Spare ribs are cut out in one piece from the inside of the belly on the underside of the pig carcass. They can be quite meaty but contain a certain amount of fat and connective tissue. Spare ribs are long and make great finger food at parties and barbecues. They contain at least 11 bones.

Flavour

The fattiness of this cut makes it ideal for barbecuing, and the meaty flavour can take on strong marinades and sauces, such as a sweet and sour sauce.

Cooking

Spare ribs are best suited to roasting, braising or barbecuing, and because of the high quantity of connective tissue they are also well suited to slow cooking in moist heat.

Also known as

Barbecue ribs, American pork ribs and enterro (Mexican). When spare ribs are trimmed into a square shape they are known as St. Louis-style ribs. If the front bone is removed they are known as Kansas City-style. Riblets are spare ribs that have been cut in half to produce short ribs; they are an economical cut designed to go further.

Leg

*The leg primal is the hind leg of the pig animal or carcass.
It is a great cut for feeding a crowd and can be prepared as
a roast, leg cutlets or steaks. It can also be cured and
smoked on the bone into ham.*

Flavour

*Cuts from the leg are fairly
lean and flavourful, though
sometimes tough. The most
tender cuts come from higher
up the leg, furthest from
the ground.*

Cooking

*Leg can be cut into roasts
and steaks for braising, slow
roasting, poaching, frying or
grilling. For roasting, choose
a leg roast that has a good
covering of fat.*

Top and bottom leg roasts and steaks

These are boneless, economical roasts and steaks. They are cut from just above the knee and are a good-value choice.

Flavour

Roasts have a good flavour though leg steaks can sometimes be a little tough because they are relatively lean. Their flavour is dependent on the amount of fat they contain and the quality of the animal they come from.

Cooking

Roasts are suitable for roasting. The steaks are best marinated to tenderise the meat before braising, frying or grilling. They can also be cut into strips for stir-fries.

Also known as

Tip roast and corner cut steaks.

Shank

The shank is the cut below the knee of the hind leg. It contains the leg bone, which is rich in gelatine and can be used to add lots of flavour and richness to stocks and stews. Shank can be cooked whole, or sliced into cross-cut steaks containing the shank bone.

Flavour

Excellent flavour when cooked correctly.

Cooking

Shank becomes meltingly tender when cooked slowly in liquid, such as braising or poaching.

Also known as

Hind shank and knuckle.

Inside and outside rounds

These are boneless cuts taken from the inside and outside of the leg.
The outside round is a little tougher and is therefore a cheaper cut.

Flavour

*Both rounds can be relatively
tender when cooked correctly.*

Cooking

*The inside round is best suited
to roasting or can be cut up for
stews and soups. The outside
round can be relatively tough
and is best suited to slow-
roasting or braising.*

Also known as

Boneless pork leg.

Offal

*Offal is cuts taken from the animal's extremities or its organs.
These cuts are also known as innards or variety meats.*

Collar bones

The small bones from the neck
of the pig are meaty and cheap to
buy. The meat is rich and chewy
and is sometimes smoked. When
simmered in soups, smoked neck
bones can be an economical
alternative to smoked ham. They
can be also be poached or braised
to add flavour to green vegetables,
stocks and stews. They are also
known as neck bones (US) and
collo (Italian).

Trotters

Pigs' feet are taken from the
bottom of the fore and hind
legs of the pig and sometimes
include part of the shank. Pigs'
feet contain little meat and
are best used in stocks to add
a rich, gelatinous flavour and
texture. They are suited to long,
slow cooking in liquid, such as
braising, and can be pickled after
cooking and eaten as a snack.
They are also known as pigs' feet
(US), *pata* (Spanish) and crubeens
(US, when cooked).

Kidneys

Like cows' kidneys, pigs' kidneys
can be relatively tough and are
best suited to long, slow cooking
in moist heat. To prepare them,
remove the outer membrane, cut
the kidneys in half and discard
the white fat in the middle. If you
find the odour or flavour of pigs'
kidneys too strong, soak them for
an hour in milk or water with a
squeeze of lemon before cooking.

Liver

Pigs' liver is strong tasting and
less desirable in cooking than
lambs' or calves' liver. It is best
soaked in milk before being
slowly cooked in liquid, by
braising, poaching or stewing.
Pigs' liver is often finely chopped
and used in forcemeats, pâtés,
sausages and terrines.

Tongue

Pork tongue should be light pink in colour. It is tough and so is suited to long, slow cooking in liquid, such as braising, poaching or stewing. Tongue is usually sold pre-cooked and sliced for sandwiches and salads.

Chitterlings

Chitterlings are the large intestines of the pig. To prepare, rinse and clean them thoroughly, then poach or stew them for up to six hours. After cooking, the tenderised chitterlings can be battered or floured and fried. Chitterlings can also be chopped up and used in sausages, for example in France's *andouillette*.

Pork casings

Pork casings are the small
intestines of the pig. They are
traditionally used to encase
sausages, although nowadays
sausage skins are often synthetic.

Heart

Fresh pig's heart should be bright
red and firm, and cheap to buy.
To prepare, rinse in cold water,
then remove any blood vessels or
clots. Pig's heart is best suited to
long, slow cooking in liquid, such
as stewing, poaching or braising,
and is often chopped up and used
in ragoûts or stews.

Pig's head

Pig's head can be stewed or braised and the meat used in terrines and pâtés. The cooked meat can also be made into brawn – sometimes known as head cheese – by being seasoned and set in a bowl with the jelly-like aspic from the cooking liquid. Brawn can be sliced for sandwiches and salads. Pig's head is also known as *tête de cochon* (French).

Cheeks

Pigs' cheeks, taken from either side of the head, can be sold as part of the head or separately. They are often cured in brine before being poached or braised until tender and can be eaten hot or cold. They are also known as chaps and *joue* (French).

Jowl

Jowl is a fatty cut taken from the face of the pig and includes all or part of the cheeks. It is often cut up and used to add flavour to stews. When jowl is cured it becomes tender and incredibly flavourful, and is considered a delicacy, particularly in Italy, where it is known as *guanciale*.

Pigs' ears, snout and tail

Pigs' ears, snout and tail are most commonly used in commercial pork meat products, such as sausages, pork pies and cold meats. They can also be boiled or stewed whole to add flavour and gelatine to stocks. Ears can be roasted and eaten as a snack or sliced into spicy Asian dishes.

Pork fat

Caul

Caul is a net of fat taken from the pig's stomach. It is wrapped around roasts to baste them as they cook. Before using, soak caul in warm water, then carefully tease it out and pat it dry. Caul is popular in Asian and Mediterranean cooking.

Back fat

Back fat is the length of firm fat taken from the upper portion of the back and shoulder of the pig, along the top of the loin primal. Sometimes back fat is still attached to the cuts it runs alongside. Alternatively, it can be removed before the loin is broken down and cut into thin sheets that are used to baste roasts. Back fat can be rendered down into lard or chopped into small studs and inserted into lean roasts to help baste them as they cook; this practice is known as larding. Back fat is also cut into small cubes and used in blood sausages (black pudding) and salami. It is also known as fatback.

Lard

Lard can be taken from any fatty tissue of the pig.
Lard taken from around the kidneys is known as
leaf lard and is used in pastries, biscuits, cakes and
for deep-frying. It is available fresh or processed;
processed lard will last longer than fresh. Lard is also
known as *lardo* (Italian) and *panne* (French).

Salt pork

Salt pork is fat taken from the belly and sides of the
pig that has been cured with salt. It contains narrow
streaks of meat and resembles very fatty bacon. Salt
pork is often sold in vacuum packs and can be added
to soups and stews for flavour and richness. For a
milder flavour, soak it in water before using. It is also
known as *petit salé* (French) and *salume* (Italian).

Cured pork

Pork was traditionally cured to preserve it. It can be made into sausages, bacon, ham and cold cuts for slicing. Cured sausage, such as German or Italian salami, Spanish chorizo and French saucisson does not need to be cooked and can be eaten cold. Pre-cooked smoked sausages, such as frankfurters, are popular in Germany and cheaper versions are used in hot dogs.

Streaky bacon

Streaky bacon is cut from the belly of the pig. It contains more fat than back bacon, and the streaked effect is caused by the meat and fat running parallel to each other. It can be cooked as whole slices or chopped up and fried with onions to add flavour to soups and stews.

Bacon

Bacon can be cut from the back (loin), side or belly of the pig. It is either dry-cured in salt and sugar or wet-cured in brine, sometimes with the addition of flavourings, such as honey or spices. Sometimes the brine solution can be injected directly into the meat to speed up the curing process; this results in a less flavoursome bacon that is more prone to shrinking when cooked, as the liquid leaches out. Bacon can be smoked after curing.

Bacon is sold in thin slices as rashers, slices or strips. The fat and skin – known as the rind – are attached to the slice. Fresh bacon should be firm and damp to the touch without being slimy and should have no odour. Avoid bacon that is streaked with silver or green; it is well past its best. Bacon is best grilled or fried and is traditionally eaten for breakfast with eggs. Pre-cooked bacon bits can also be used as toppings for pizzas and salads.

Back bacon

Back bacon is cut from the back (loin) of the pig. It is relatively lean, meaty and firmly textured and can be thickly sliced into bacon steaks for grilling, frying or roasting.

Lardons

Lardons are small cubes of thickly cut bacon, usually taken from the belly of the pig. They can be fried, often with sliced onions, to flavour soups, stews, quiches and risottos. They can also be fried until crisp and sprinkled over salads to give flavour and texture.

Pancetta

Pancetta is Italian air-dried bacon cut from belly of pork. It can be smoked and sold either as one whole piece or cut into thin slices or cubes for frying. Pancetta has a concentrated flavour and endless culinary uses: it can be chopped into soups, stews and pasta dishes; whole slices can be wrapped around chicken and fish before roasting; or it can be fried until crisp and sprinkled over salads.

Prosciutto

Prosciutto is the Italian word for ham and it can be either *crudo* (raw) or *cotto* (cooked). The ham is preserved by curing and air-drying for up to two years before being cut into wafer-thin slices and served as part of an antipasto or in salads. Prosciutto can be made all over Italy but *prosciutto di Parma* is the best-known (see right).

Parma ham

True Parma ham must come from a certain breed of pig in Parma. The ham is cured with a mix of dry and wet salt. This is a slow process and its production is subject to strict monitoring and controls. The meat is delicate and flavoursome and is usually eaten cold as an antipasto. If Parma ham is left on the bone it will continue to mature and develop in flavour.

Salami

Salami is a firm sausage made from finely chopped fat and meat – often pork – plus seasonings, such as garlic, peppercorns and herbs. It is usually cured or brined and sometimes smoked. Salami can be sliced and eaten cold or cooked into stews and sauces. Pepperoni is an American take on salami, often used on pizza toppings or in sandwiches.

Chorizo

Chorizo is a spiced sausage, popular in Spain and Portugal (where it is known as *chouriço*). It is made from chopped meat – pork or beef – and fat, and is seasoned with a variety of ingredients, including smoked paprika, which provides its distinctive red colour and smoky flavour. Chorizo is air-dried and sometimes smoked. It can range from mild to spicy in flavour and can be sliced and eaten cold, tapas-style, or cooked into stews and sauces.

Techniques

Scoring fat on a pork roast

Scoring the top fat on a roast of pork before roasting will produce delicious, crisp crackling and helps the fat to baste and tenderise the meat as it cooks.

First, make sure the rind is completely dry; pat it dry with kitchen towel if it is damp or wet.

Using a sharp knife, score through the rind evenly at 5mm (¼in) intervals in a criss-cross pattern.

Rub salt and olive oil into the slashes. You may wish to flavour the roast further by rubbing in extra ingredients, such as garlic, lemon zest or herbs.

Weigh the pork, put it onto a trivet in a roasting tin and roast according to the calculated cooking time until the crackling is crisp and golden and the meat is cooked through. Remove the crackling before carving the meat, and snap it into pieces.

Preparing and cooking pork medallions

Medallions are round slices of boneless meat
that are tender enough to be fried or grilled.
Pork medallions can be cut from the tenderloin;
one tenderloin will serve two to three people.

Remove the silver membrane that runs along the
top of the tenderloin.

Cut the tenderloin into 2.5cm- (1in-) thick slices.
Cover the slices with wet plastic wrap or non-
stick baking parchment and bat out with a meat
tenderiser. Season with salt and pepper.

Heat a little oil in a large frying pan and fry the
medallions for 2 to 3 minutes on each side until
golden and cooked through – do this in batches
if necessary. Remove the medallions from the pan
to make a pan sauce (see page 182), then return to
the pan to heat through just before serving.

Making a pan sauce for pork

Using the cooking juices to make a rich, flavoursome sauce adds lots of extra flavour to the finished dish and can easily be done while the meat is resting.

When the meat is cooked, remove it from the pan, cover with foil and let it rest in a warm place. Drain away any excess fat from the pan, then add a splash of wine, stock or cider. Put the pan back over a low heat and use a spatula to scrape up any browned, caramelized pieces stuck to the bottom; this is where all the flavour is.

Gradually add a good-quality hot stock, stirring constantly, until the liquid is bubbling. You may wish to flavour it further with additional ingredients, such as mushrooms, chopped onions, herbs or mustard. Once the liquid is starting to thicken, add a splash of cream. Return the meat to the pan to warm through with the sauce or serve the sauce poured over the meat.

Cooking pigs' trotters

Remove any hair from the trotters – the easiest way to do this is to singe the hairs off. Soak the trotters in cold water in the refrigerator for 24 hours. Remove from the water and put them into a large deep-sided pan with chopped vegetables, such as carrot, onion and celery. Add a bouquet garni and enough cold water to cover them. Bring to the boil and simmer for 3 to 4 hours, topping up with water as necessary, until the feet are tender. Cool in the liquid, then remove with a slotted spoon. They should split in half quite easily. The cooked trotters may then be floured and fried or grilled for extra flavour.

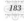

Preparing a suckling pig for roasting

To prepare, slash through the skin and fat all over the pig, except the head. Make a herb rub by mixing salt, chopped fresh herbs, grated lemon zest and black pepper. Rub into the cavity of the pig and into the slashes, then keep in a cool place for up to 24 hours to allow the flavours to develop.

Preheat the oven to 200°C (400°F/Gas mark 6). Weigh the pig and calculate the cooking time at 15 minutes per 450g (1lb). Put the pig, belly side down, onto a trivet or wire rack in a large roasting tin (the trivet will allow the hot air to circulate freely and the meat to cook evenly). Cover the snout and ears with foil to keep them from burning and brush the pig all over with oil. Roast for 20 to 30 minutes, then lower the temperature to 175°C (350°F/Gas mark 4) and roast for the calculated time, basting regularly with the juices, until golden on the outside and cooked through. Suckling pig can be served hot or cold. It is also known as *cochon de lait* (French) and piglet.

Suckling pigs are unweaned piglets that have been slaughtered at between two and four weeks of age. The meat is pale and tender and is served with the golden, crispy crackling skin. Allow one suckling pig to serve around 10 people.

Marinating ribs for the barbecue

To make a tasty marinade for ribs, put some grated
ginger, minced garlic, honey, lemon juice, hoisin
sauce and chopped herbs in a pan. Heat gently,
stirring, to dissolve the honey. Leave to cool, then
rub the marinade into the ribs. Marinate in the
refrigerator for at least 1 hour in a non-metallic
dish or a resealable plastic bag. The thinner the
marinade, the faster it will penetrate the meat; the
thinner the ribs, the faster the marinade will take
hold. Baste the ribs with barbecue sauce as they
cook, for extra flavour.

Testing pork for doneness

A meat thermometer is an inexpensive investment for accurately testing the doneness of meat. A meat thermometer may be placed in the thickest part of the raw meat before cooking, so you can check the temperature without opening the oven door. Alternatively, it can be inserted into the roast just before the calculated cooking time is up. Transfer the roast to a board and push a meat thermometer into its thickest part; hold for 15 seconds. Pork should be cooked until well-done, with a minimum core temperature of 75°F (170°C), but remove it from the oven just before it reaches this, because the meat will carry on cooking as it rests.

Carving a bone-in loin of pork

Remove the roast from the oven and put it onto a warmed plate. Cover it with foil and rest it in a warm place for up to 30 minutes.

Transfer the roast to a carving board. Using a sharp carving knife, cut carefully between the meat and the crackling. Remove the crackling and cut it into small pieces along the scored marks.

Cut along the length of the roast to remove the backbone. Sit the roast on this flattened edge, then carve between the rib bones to separate them into pieces. For smaller slices, slice more thinly so that every other piece contains a rib bone. Alternatively, tease the meat from the bones, then slice it off, leaving the bones in place. Arrange the slices on a warmed serving platter with the crackling.

Pork and lentil stew

This is a robust one-pot dish that uses a shoulder cut of pork and is incredibly simple to prepare.

Serves 6

450g (1lb) green or
brown lentils
2 onions, chopped
1 carrot, chopped
4 garlic cloves, halved
lengthways
1 red pepper, deseeded
and chopped
225g ½lb black pudding
225g (½lb) chorizo
225g (½lb) fresh picnic
shoulder, cut into chunks
1 bay leaf, torn in half
A few parsley sprigs
2 tbsp olive oil

Put all the ingredients into a heavy cooking pot. Add enough water to cover by about 2.5cm (1in), then bring to a boil. Simmer gently for 30 to 40 minutes, topping up with water when necessary, until the meat and lentils are tender and the liquid has almost evaporated.

Remove the black pudding and chorizo. Slice, and return to the stew. Mix well, then serve with rice or potatoes.

Stir-fried minced pork

This speedy dish is a great way to add lots of flavour to minced pork. Serve with noodles or rice.

Serves 4–6

Put all the ingredients for the marinade into a small pan and heat gently for 5 minutes, stirring. Cool, then mix into the minced pork. Set aside to marinate.

Heat the oil in a large frying pan or wok. Add the garlic, fry for 1 minute, then add the marinated pork. Fry over a high heat for 3 minutes, stirring constantly, then add the olives, mushrooms and chilli. Stir-fry for 3 minutes or until the pork is cooked.

250g (9oz) minced pork
1 tbsp groundnut oil
1 tsp minced garlic
1 tbsp black olives,
finely chopped
225g (½lb) button mushrooms,
sliced
1 red chilli, finely sliced

For the marinade:

1 tsp cornflour
2 tsp light soy sauce
1 tsp sugar
1 tsp rice wine
2 tbsp groundnut oil

Roast pork with apple–walnut stuffing

This is a simple yet elegant dish using pork loin. The crunch of walnuts, touch of spice and the sweetness of the sultanas go perfectly with the succulent meat.

Serves 8

6 tbsp butter, chopped
2 large, tart apples, peeled,
cored and cut into
1cm (½-in) chunks
1 small onion, chopped
2 celery stalks, chopped
1 garlic clove, finely chopped
170g (6oz) soft breadcrumbs
110g (4oz) walnut pieces
85g (3oz) sultanas
¼ tsp ground cloves
½ tsp mustard powder
1 boneless pork loin roast,
weighing about 1.5kg (3lb)
3 tbsp vegetable oil

To make the stuffing, melt 3 tbsp butter in a medium frying pan. Add the apples and fry for 8 to 10 minutes until soft. Tip into a large bowl and set aside. Add the remaining butter to the pan and fry the onion, celery and garlic for 5 minutes until softened. Add to the apples with the breadcrumbs, walnuts, sultanas, cloves and mustard. Season with salt and mix well. If the mixture is very firm add a splash of milk to loosen it. Set aside.

Preheat the oven to 190°C (375°F/Gas mark 5).

Cut the pork almost in half lengthways. Flatten it out and make slashes lengthways along its thickest parts. Spoon the stuffing over the pork, pressing into the slashes. Carefully bring up the sides of the roast and tightly tie into a roll. Push any stuffing back into the roast as you tie it.

Heat the oil in a large frying pan. Add the pork and sauté quickly until golden all over. Transfer the meat to a board, placing it on top of four lengths of kitchen string.
Weigh the stuffed roast and calculate the cooking time at 25 minutes per 450g (1lb). Put the stuffed roast onto a trivet in a roasting pan and roast according to the calculated cooking time or until cooked through. Leave the pork to rest for 15 minutes before carving.

Pork with cabbage and corn

This is a hearty one-pot pork rib dish that's full of flavour. If you can't get hold of fresh corn, frozen is fine.

Serves 6

Put the pork ribs into a heavy cooking pot. Add just enough water to cover, then cook on the hob over a medium heat for 1 to 1½ hours or until the meat is tender. Add the onion and tomatoes and cook for a further 10 minutes.

Blend the garlic, cumin, peppercorns and vinegar in a food processor. Add to the pork mixture with the cabbage and sweetcorn. Stir well and season. Cook for 5 minutes or until the cabbage is just tender. Serve with rice.

700g (1½lb) pork loin
ribs, chopped
1 medium onion, sliced
2 large tomatoes, sliced
2 garlic cloves
A pinch of cumin seeds
8 peppercorns
2 tbsp vinegar
1 medium cabbage, sliced
350g (12oz) sweetcorn

Spiced pork and aubergine chop suey

This spiced Chinese-style dish of marinated pork tenderloin and crisp vegetables is delicious served with rice or noodles.

Serves 4

1 pork tenderloin, weighing about 450g (1lb), trimmed and thinly sliced
700g (1½lb) mixed stir-fry vegetables, such as carrots, peppers, mange tout and beansprouts
1 aubergine, halved lengthways and sliced thinly
4 tbsp groundnut oil

For the marinade:

5cm (2in) piece ginger, roughly grated
2 garlic cloves, crushed
1 tbsp five-spice powder
1 fresh green chilli, deseeded and finely chopped
4 tbsp soy sauce
1 tbsp chilli sauce
1 tbsp light brown sugar

To make the marinade, squeeze the juice from the grated ginger and mix with the remaining marinade ingredients. Add the pork and toss to coat in the mixture. Marinate for 1 hour, turning occasionally.

Meanwhile, cut the vegetables into 5cm (2in) lengths. Heat the oil in a wok or large frying pan until almost smoking, then add the marinated pork with the aubergine. Stir-fry for 4 to 5 minutes until golden, then add the remaining vegetables and any remaining marinade. Cook until liquid is very hot and simmering, then serve immediately with rice or noodles.

Tolosa red bean stew with pork

This pork belly dish is from Tolosa in the Spanish Basque country, a region famous for its love of red beans and highly seasoned sausages like chorizo.

Serves 4

Drain the beans and put them in a pot with the pork and half the chopped onion. Add 1 tablespoon of oil and cover with water. Bring to the boil, turn down the heat, cover and simmer gently for 2 hours or until the meat is almost tender. Check regularly that the water level remains high enough, adding more if necessary to stop the stew from drying out.

Fry the ham fat to give off grease, or heat the oil in a pan. Slice the chorizos and fry them with the chopped pepper.

Remove the pork or bacon from the beans and chop it into cubes. Check the amount of liquid in the pot: it should now be well reduced (if not, pour some off). Add all the meats to the pot and season everything well.

Fry the remaining onion in the same pan you used for the sausage, adding the garlic at the end. Stir into the beans and simmer 10 minutes more, then serve.

450g (1lb) red beans,
soaked overnight
150g (5oz) pork belly or
boiling bacon, in one piece
1 large onion, finely chopped
2 tbsp olive oil
2 tbsp chopped ham fat or
more olive oil
2 chorizo sausages
1 large green pepper, deseeded
and chopped
Salt and freshly ground
black pepper
2 garlic cloves, finely chopped

Roasted spare ribs with lemongrass and chilli

This is a simple and tasty Asian-style way to add flavour to spare ribs.
Serves 4–6

Wash and dry the spare ribs and put them in a large bowl.

In another bowl, combine the honey, five-spice powder, garlic, dry sherry, fish sauce, lemongrass and chilli. Mix well. Spread the honey mixture over the spare ribs and leave to marinate for 4 hours.

12 pork spare ribs
2 tbsp clear honey
1 tsp five-spice powder
2 cloves garlic, minced
3 tbsp dry sherry or rice wine
3 tbsp fish sauce or 3 tbsp light
soy sauce mixed with 1 tsp
anchovy essence
2 stalks fresh lemongrass,
thinly sliced
2 fresh red chillies,
finely chopped

The ribs can be grilled on a barbecue, turning frequently and basting with the marinade; baked in an oven preheated to 160°C (325°F/Gas mark 3); or cooked under a moderately hot grill, basting regularly with the marinade.

Roast pork Puerto Rican-style

This is a great way of cooking a leg of pork. It's a favourite dish in Puerto Rico where it is loved for its spicy flavours.
Serves 8–10

Fry the garlic in the olive oil for 1 minute. Tip into a food processor and blend to a paste with the oregano, cumin, spring onions, coriander, pepper and rum. Season with salt and pepper.

Put the leg of pork into a roasting tin. Score the top of the roast into a diamond pattern, cutting through the rind and fat. Rub the garlic paste into the slashes, cover and marinate overnight in the refrigerator.

Preheat the oven to 160°C (325°F/Gas mark 3).

Unwrap the pork and roast in the oven for 2 hours. Add the potatoes, onions and squash to the roasting tin and baste with the fat. Roast for 1 hour, then add the courgette and baste with the fat. Roast for a further 45 minutes until the meat is cooked through and the vegetables are tender. Transfer the meat to a carving board, cover loosely with foil and leave to rest for 15 minutes. Arrange the vegetables in a serving dish and keep warm.

To make the gravy, pour the excess fat from the roasting tin into a container and discard. Sprinkle the flour over the drippings in the roasting tin and stir over a medium heat until smooth, scraping up any browned bits from the bottom of the tin. Gradually beat in the beef stock or water until blended. Bring to the boil, reduce the heat and simmer for 5 minutes or until thickened, stirring occasionally. Slice the pork and serve with the vegetables and gravy.

1 tbsp minced garlic
3 tbsp olive oil
½ tsp dried oregano
leaves, finely crumbled
¾ tsp ground cumin
4 spring onions, chopped
1 large bunch
coriander, chopped
1 green pepper, deseeded
and chopped
250ml (8fl oz) white rum
1 leg of pork, weighing about
3kg (7lb) with bone
2 large baking potatoes,
scrubbed and cut into wedges
2 large red onions, cut
into wedges
½ butternut squash, peeled
and cut into 2.5cm (1in) slices
3 courgettes, cut into
2.5cm (1in) slices

For the gravy:

4 tbsp fat from dripping in
roasting tin
25g (1oz) flour
1l (30fl oz) beef stock or water

Explosive-fried kidney with coriander

Explosive-frying involves cooking with very intense heat and is particularly suitable for ingredients with a delicate texture.

Serves 4

4 pigs' kidneys
2 pieces pork stomach
2 tbsp cornflour
2 tbsp groundnut oil
1 tsp chopped garlic
1 large bunch coriander stalks,
cut into 4cm (1½in) lengths
8 tbsp hot chicken stock
1 tbsp soy sauce
1 tsp Chinese rice wine
1 tsp toasted sesame oil

Split the kidneys in half, remove the fat, membrane and gristle, and rub with 1 tbsp salt. Wash them thoroughly and soak for 30 minutes.

Split the stomach and rub all over with 1 tbsp salt. Wash and rub it with the cornflour until it is completely clean. Score into a diamond pattern and cut it into slices. Drain the kidneys and cut into slices.

Heat the oil in a large pan and add the garlic, kidneys and stomach, stirring over a very high heat for 30 seconds. Add the coriander stalks and chicken stock and bring to a boil. Drain off the stock and add the soy sauce, rice wine and toasted sesame oil, stir-frying over a very high heat for 20 seconds. Serve immediately.

Pig trotter stew

This simple Vietnamese dish is packed with flavour and requires little preparation.

Serves 4

*2 lb pigs' trotters, washed,
blanched and chopped into
5cm (2in) pieces
1.2l (40fl oz) chicken or
pork stock
1 large onion, sliced
3 boiled potatoes, quartered
3 tomatoes, diced
50g (2oz) green beans, sliced
100g (4oz) beansprouts
3 tbsp chopped spring onions,
to garnish*

For the Vietnamese bouquet garni:

*2 large celery stalks with
leaves, roughly chopped
3 large bunches coriander,
including stalks, plus
extra to garnish
2 large lemongrass
stalks, chopped
6 large garlic cloves,
finely chopped
1 cinnamon stick
2 star anise
1 tbsp black peppercorns*

Wrap the ingredients for the bouquet garni in a square of muslin and tie into a bundle with string.

Put the trotters into a large pan. Cover with water, bring to the boil and simmer for 2 to 3 hours or until the meat comes away from the bone. Drain, then tip back into the pan with the stock and enough water to cover the trotters. Bring to the boil, add the bouquet garni to the pot and simmer for 10 minutes or until the liquid is slightly thickened.

Add the onion, potatoes and tomatoes and simmer for 5 minutes. Add the beans and cook for 2 minutes, until tender. Add the beansprouts and remove the bouquet garni. Sprinkle with the extra coriander and chopped spring onions, then serve immediately.

LAMB

Lamb is the meat taken from a young sheep that has been slaughtered in the first year of its life. Because the animal is young when slaughtered, most cuts are relatively tender and delicate. The texture and flavour of lamb responds well to marinating, and cuts can be roasted, fried, grilled or slow-cooked in moist heat. Meat from a sheep over one year old is known as hogget; mutton refers to the meat taken from a sheep over two years old.

Rack

Shoulder

Foreshank

Primal cuts

The primal cuts are those made in the initial stage of butchering. They may be sold whole, or subdivided into smaller cuts for sale to home cooks.

Loin

Leg

Breast

Shoulder

The shoulder primal of the sheep carcass is an economical cut, albeit relatively fatty and bony. When cooked slowly, the fatty network breaks down and tenderises the meat.

Flavour

Great flavour when cooked slowly.

Cooking

Shoulder cuts are best suited to slow cooking in liquid, such as braising or stewing, to break down the connective tissue.

Neck

Cuts from the neck can be bone-in or boneless fillets.

Flavour

The neck is naturally quite tough as it is worked hard by the animal, however it has great flavour when cooked slowly.

Cooking

Cuts from the neck are best slowly cooked in liquid, such as braising or stewing, to break down the connective tissue. Cook them on the bone for extra flavour and texture. Cuts from the neck are traditionally used in Lancashire hotpot and in Irish stew.

Also known as

Lamb neck fillets, scrag end, stewing lamb, middle neck and lamb neck pieces.

Round- or square-cut shoulder roast and boneless rolled shoulder

This large, round or square-shaped cut can be bone-in or boneless; if the bones remain in (the shoulder blade, arm bone and up to seven ribs), it can be sliced into blade chops. The roast is far easier to carve if you ask your butcher to remove the bones first. With the bones removed it is sold as boneless shoulder or boneless rolled shoulder for stews and curries.

Flavour

Good flavour when cooked correctly.

Cooking

Boneless rolled shoulder roast is well suited to marinating and stuffing before roasting. Shoulder responds best to roasting at a slightly lower temperature for a little longer. Blade chops are best suited to braising.

Also known as

Round cut, shoulder roast, lamb round- or square-cut shoulder and shoulder block.

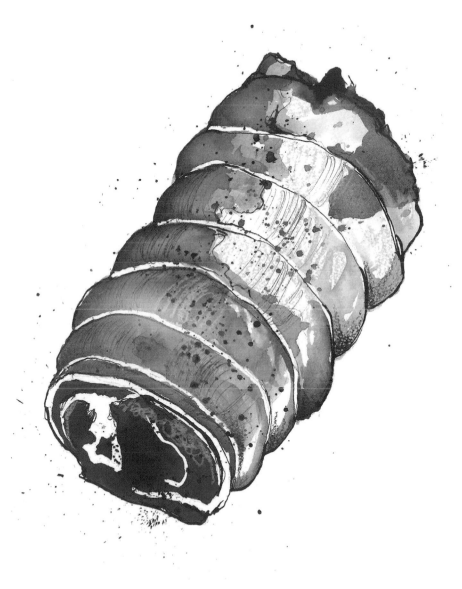

Blade chops

These are economical chops cut from the shoulder blade.

Flavour

The ratio of fat to meat gives these a good flavour.

Cooking

Blade chops are best grilled, roasted, fried or braised.

Also known as

Shoulder chops, shoulder blade chops and shoulder blade lamb chops.

Fore shank

This is the fore leg of the sheep, taken from the lower end of the shoulder primal. It is a smaller cut than the hind shank.

Flavour

Lamb shank is relatively lean, but it becomes tender and flavourful when cooked slowly.

Cooking

It is best suited to long, slow cooking such as braising to break down the connective tissue. The meat from the shank can also be minced or cut into cubes for stews. Lamb shanks can also replace veal shanks in osso buco.

Also known as

Lamb shank, lamb trotter and shin.

Breast

Lamb breast is cut from the forequarter of the sheep and includes part of the belly. Lamb spare ribs are cut from here.

Flavour

Breast is a relatively fatty cut, streaked with fat. It is sweet-tasting and flavourful.

Cooking

It is best suited to stuffing and roasting, braising, barbecuing or pot-roasting.

Also known as

Poitrine d'agneau *(French).*

Flavour

Spare ribs are full of flavour though they can be somewhat fatty.

Cooking

Spare ribs are best marinated then grilled or braised.

Also known as

If the spare ribs are cut into long, skinny individual ribs, they are known as riblets; originally this was an economical way of making them go further.

Spare ribs

Lamb breast spare ribs are cut from the breast primal and contain the rib bones with the meat and fat in between.

Rack

This is an expensive primal and makes an impressive roast to serve at the table. Rack of lamb consists of eight rib bones, backbone and the rib-eye muscle. It slices easily into tender chops and cutlets. A crown roast is made by curving and tying two racks together into a circle and sitting them upright on the backbone. A guard of honour is made by criss-crossing two racks together.

Flavour

Succulent, tender and sweet, thanks to the rib bones.

Cooking

Rack of lamb is best suited to roasting. Chops and cutlets can be grilled or barbecued.

Also known as

Best end, rib roast. Boneless cuts from the best end are known as cannons and carrés d'agneau (French). Cannon of lamb is a boneless fillet taken from the rack.

Rib chops and cutlets

Rib chops are cut from the rib roast. If the fat is trimmed away from the end of the bone they are known as having been Frenched. If the chine bone (backbone) has been removed they are described as chined.

Flavour

They are tender, meaty and sweet, thanks to the rib-eye muscle and rib bones.

Cooking

Rib chops are best suited to grilling, frying, roasting and barbecuing.

Loin

Cuts from the loin primal are expensive, tender and flavourful. The loin primal contains the chine bone, but this can be removed to create a boneless roast which is ideal for stuffing, rolling and tying. It can also be cut into lean, boneless pieces called noisettes.

Flavour

Cuts from the loin are succulent and juicy, thanks to the extra fat for basting.

Cooking

Larger cuts from the loin are best suited to roasting. Noisettes can be fried or grilled. Lamb loin chops can be fried, grilled or barbecued.

Loin roast and saddle of lamb

The loin roast is cut from the loin primal. A saddle of lamb consists of the two loin roasts, one from each side of the sheep carcass, joined together by the backbone. It makes an impressive roast and is ideal for serving a crowd, although it is an expensive choice.

Flavour

Tender, succulent and flavourful.

Cooking

The loins can be roasted whole.

Also known as

Loin roll, boneless loin roast, rolled lamb roast (if the bone is removed). A saddle of lamb is also known as double loin roll or rolled double lamb roast if the bone is removed.

Loin chops and double loin chops

Loin chops are an expensive cut. They contain the eye of the loin and the chine bone (backbone). Double loin chops are cut across the backbone and are generous in size. They consist of the top loin and fillet. The bone can be removed and the chops cut and rolled into boneless chops known as noisettes of lamb.

Flavour

Lean and flavoursome.

Cooking

Loin and double loin chops are best suited to grilling or frying. Double loin chops can also be roasted.

Also known as

T-bone chops, Barnsley chops, centre loin chops (Irish).

Strip loin

The strip loin is a boneless strip cut from the loin. It consists of the loin eye muscle and is an expensive cut.

Flavour

This is a lean and tender cut.

Cooking

It is best suited to gentle cooking, such as braising or slow roasting.

Also known as

Boneless loin. The strip loin can also be called cannon, similar to the one cut from the rack.

Fillet and medallions

The slim fillet can be cut into slices called medallions. One lamb fillet will serve just one person. Because it is so small, it is usually left attached to the strip loin.

Flavour

Incredibly tender and flavoursome.

Cooking

Fillet is often rolled in herbs and spices before being roasted or fried.

Also known as

Tenderloin.

Leg

***The leg primal cut is the hind leg of the sheep or carcass.
It is relatively expensive and can be cut in half, if required,
into the larger shank and the smaller top end.***

The leg bone can be removed and the boned meat can then be stuffed, rolled and tied, or slashed open on both sides to increase the surface area (butterflied) for roasting, grilling or barbecuing. The leg can be cut into numerous mini roasts and can also be cut into cubes for stewing, braising or kebabs.

Flavour

*Leg is lean, yet succulent
and flavoursome when
cooked correctly.*

Cooking

*Cuts from the leg can be
roasted or cooked slowly
in liquid, such as braising,
stewing or pot-roasting.*

Shank

The shank is the lower part of the leg from the knee to the ankle. Some shanks can be cut more generously to include part of the loin from higher up the leg.

Flavour

Tender and flavoursome when cooked slowly.

Cooking

The lower shank section is best suited to long, slow cooking in liquid, such as braising, stewing or pot-roasting.

Also known as

Knuckle of lamb and shank of lamb.

Top end

The top end of leg can be bone-in or boned. It is good value and makes a popular roast for a gathering. If the hip bone has been removed it is easier to carve. A centre leg roast is a leg of lamb with the shank taken off at the knee. Centre leg slices may be cut from here.

Flavour
Leg of lamb is lean and tender.

Cooking
It is best suited to roasting and is best served pink; it can dry out if overcooked.

Also known as
Centre cut lamb leg.

Boneless leg roast

This leg roast is boned, trimmed, rolled and tied.

Flavour

It has great flavour due to its natural coating of fat, which bastes the tender meat as it cooks. Sometimes the fat is removed, in which case it is a relatively lean cut.

Cooking

Best suited to searing over a high heat, then roasting

Chump roast and chump chops

The chump roast is cut from the top of the leg where it meets the loin and can be bone-in or boneless. Chump chops can be cut from here; further down the leg they become leg steaks. One chump roast will feed two people.

Flavour

Relatively lean but still tender and meaty.

Cooking

Take care not to overcook because it can dry out easily.

Also known as

Foremost section of the leg.

Flavour

Flavoursome when cooked correctly.

Cooking

Chops are best suited to braising and grilling. Take care not to overcook because they can dry out easily.

Also known as

Lamb leg chops and lamb leg steaks.

Round leg chops and steaks

These can be cut into bone-in or boneless chops and steaks.

Offal

Offal is cuts taken from the extremities of the animal or the organs within. They are also known as innards or variety meats.

Liver

Lambs' liver is less tender and a little stronger in flavour than calves' liver. It is pink and smooth-textured and can be fried in butter with bacon and onions, grilled or braised. Lambs' liver is one of the key ingredients in the traditional Scottish dish haggis. It is also known as lambs' fry.

Kidneys

Lambs' kidneys are single-lobed. Always make sure they are as fresh as possible because they can deteriorate rapidly. Lambs' kidneys are particularly good fried with bacon.

Sweetbreads

Sweetbreads is the name given
to the delicately flavoured
thymus glands in the throat and
the pancreas in the stomach of
the sheep. Lambs' sweetbreads
are usually cheaper than calves'
and rarely less tender; those
from mutton are tougher and
less edible than lambs'. They
are particularly good fried with
lambs' brains and liver.
See page 237 for how to
prepare sweetbreads.

Heart

Fresh lambs' heart should be
red and firm. To prepare, rinse
in cold water then remove any
blood vessels or clots. Hearts
are best suited to long, slow
cooking in liquid, such as stewing
or braising, until they become
tender. Lambs' heart is one of the
key ingredients in the traditional
Scottish dish haggis.

Tongue

Lamb's tongue is relatively small. It is best cooked by poaching in stock until tender, before being skinned. It can then be pickled, set into a cold jelly or fried.

Lungs

Lambs' lungs are bright pink, soft and spongy and are one of the key ingredients in the traditional Scottish dish haggis. They are also known as lights.

Brains

Lambs' brains should be plump
and fresh. To prepare, remove
any visible clots, then soak in
cold water, changing the water
frequently. Poach briefly in
water and vinegar, then either
eat them cold in a vinaigrette
or flour and fry them with herbs
until sweet-tasting and creamy
textured. Lambs' brains are
particularly popular in European
and Lebanese dishes.

Testicles

Lambs' testicles are small
and pale pink in colour, with
a soft, creamy texture, and a
mild, delicate flavour when
cooked. Eaten on ranches in
the American West and in the
Middle East, lambs' testicles are
considered a forgotten delicacy
by some. They are sold skinned
and ready for cooking by frying,
and are commonly known as
lamb fries.

Meat from sheep of different ages

Suckling lamb

Suckling lamb is lamb that has been slaughtered up to five weeks of age, has only ever been fed on its mother's milk, and has never grazed outdoors. As a consequence, its meat is pale, delicate and tender. Suckling lamb is usually roasted whole and makes a great feast for a crowd; sometimes suckling lambs are spit-roasted for religious celebrations and festivals. It is also known as milk-fed lamb and baby lamb.

Spring lamb

The main lambing season is in the spring, but spring lamb sold at this time is not lambs born in the spring, because they would be far too young; instead, spring lamb refers to lambs born the previous November and December that are just about old enough for slaughtering in the spring. Spring lamb is often intensively reared for the Easter market by being kept indoors on a controlled diet. It is also known as Easter lamb.

Hogget

A sheep that is slaughtered between one and two years of age is known
as hogget. Meat from a hogget is more strongly flavoured than lamb.
Shoulder of hogget can be slow-roasted, braised or stewed until tender.

Mutton

A sheep that is at least two years old is known as mutton. The carcass
requires aging by hanging. Mutton is a darker, more flavourful and
fattier meat than lamb. Cuts from the leg, shoulder, loin or neck are most
commonly used. Mutton becomes tender when slow-roasted or braised or
simmered into a broth.

Techniques

Open-boning and butterflying a leg of lamb

To remove the bone, use a long-bladed boning knife and hold it like a dagger, pointing the tip downwards as you cut through the meat. Start at the knuckle end and cut through the firmer side of the leg, following the bone closely, until you can work it out of the meat. The bone should lift out (reserve it for making a stock), leaving you with a boneless leg of lamb.

Butterflying opens out and flattens a piece of boneless meat, increasing its surface area for absorbing flavours, such as marinades, helping it to cook quickly and evenly, and making it easy to carve. Butterfly joints are usually applied to leg cuts. Lay the boned leg out on a board. You may wish to remove some of the fat from the outside of the leg, leaving just a thin covering. Then, following the natural grain, make slashes through the meat at regular intervals all over, using a sharp knife. Turn the meat over and repeat on the other side, taking care not to cut all the way through from one slash to another. The idea is to flatten the meat out as evenly as possible. Butterflied leg of lamb can be marinated before being grilled or barbecued.

Preparing a rack of lamb

To prepare for roasting, lift the skin from one
corner and pull it up and across the fat and meat
to remove it – it should come away in one piece.
The chine bone (backbone) also needs to be removed
and discarded, if your butcher has not already
done so. You will need to do this with a small saw,
separating the chine bone from the rib bones, until
it comes away.

Next, use a sharp knife to cut away the piece
of cartilage that sits within the meat and fat at
the thinner end of the rack; remove it with your
fingers. Also remove the rubbery tendon that lies
between the fat and meat. Turn the rack over so
it is fat side up. Make a horizontal cut across the
fat, approximately 2.5cm (1in) from the tips of the
bones. Remove the fat to expose the ends of the
bones, then cut between each bone, trimming and
scraping the bones to remove all the fat, to expose
the tips of the bones. Finally, carefully cut away the
fat covering the back of the rack so that only a thin
layer remains.

The rack of lamb may be roasted whole or chopped
into cutlets and grilled or fried until tender and just
pink inside.

Preparing a guard of honour

A guard of honour is made by interlocking the rib bones of two prepared racks of lamb.

Place each prepared rack of lamb flat side down on a board so they face each other, with the bones pointing upwards. Holding one in each hand, push the racks together, so the bones interlock in a criss-cross fashion.

Using kitchen string, tie down through the guard of honour at regular intervals to hold the racks together.

Assembling a crown roast

A crown roast is made from two prepared racks of lamb that are curved and tied together into a circle and roasted.

To assemble a crown roast, hold each rack flat-side down and bend each into a semi-circle with the fat on the inside (if the rack is too rigid to bend, make a small cut between each cutlet to give it a little more flexibility). Using a thick needle and thread, sew the racks together vertically down each side to form a circle. Tie some string around the 'waist' of the crown to secure it further.

Before roasting, a crown roast is traditionally stuffed with a stuffing such as breadcrumbs and herbs.

To serve, slice into cutlets and serve each with a little of the stuffing.

Preparing a saddle of lamb for roasting

Two loins that are still joined together
are known as a saddle of lamb. This cut
makes a great roast that will easily serve
10 to 12 people.

To prepare, cut away any excess fat from
underneath the saddle and around the edges.
Remove the kidneys.

Place the saddle on a board, back-fat side up.
The hip (aitch) bone should be protruding from one
end. Using a small, sharp knife, lift the skin from
one corner of the saddle and pull it up and across
the fat and meat to remove it – it should come away
in one piece. Discard the skin, then score the back
fat evenly all over in a criss-cross fashion.

Testing lamb for doneness

Lamb should be cooked until at least
medium-rare – that is, until at least slightly
pink and without any traces of blood – with
a core temperature of 55–60°C (130–140°F).
Insert a meat thermometer into the meat
before roasting – so you can check the
temperature without opening the oven door
– or test when the roast is almost cooked. To
take an accurate reading, the thermometer
should be inserted into the thickest part
of the meat and held for 15 seconds. If the
thermometer is inserted before roasting,
remove the roast just before it reaches 55°C
(130°F), because the meat will carry on
cooking while it rests.

Preparing kidneys

Lambs' kidneys are single-lobed and are relatively straightforward to prepare. First remove the outer membrane and any blood vessels. Cut in half and remove the central fatty core, then rinse in cold water. Lambs' kidneys may be fried or grilled until just pink inside, or cooked slowly in liquid, such as in a braise or stew.

Preparing sweetbreads

Lambs' sweetbreads are not considered such a
delicacy as calves' sweetbreads, but they make a
tasty dish nonetheless. Both types of sweetbreads
– from the thymus gland and from the stomach –
can be prepared by repeatedly soaking in fresh
water, until they turn white. Blanch the soaked
sweetbreads in boiling, salted water for 1 to 2
minutes, drain, then refresh under cold water.
Press them dry with a clean dish towel, dust with
flour and fry until hot and creamy inside. Blanched
sweetbreads can also be roasted, braised or gently
poached in an aromatic broth for 45 minutes or
until tender.

Fried lamb with paprika and vinegar

This garlic-spiked dish using shoulder of lamb is quick to make and full of spicy flavours.
Serves 4

1 slice stale bread
3 tbsp red wine vinegar
3 tbsp olive oil
800g (1¾ lb) lean lamb
shoulder, diced
6 garlic cloves, minced
½ dried chilli,
deseeded and sliced
1 tbsp paprika
½ tsp ground cloves
4 tbsp finely chopped parsley

Sprinkle the bread with the vinegar. Heat 2 tbsp oil in a large frying pan or heavy cooking pot and fry the bread for 3 to 4 minutes until golden. Remove from the pan and set aside.

Add the remaining oil, lamb, half the garlic and the chilli to the pan and fry over a high heat, stirring constantly, for 10 minutes or until the lamb is golden. Add the paprika, cloves, remaining garlic, parsley and 200ml (7fl oz) water. Cover and cook for 30 minutes or until the lamb is tender and the liquid has reduced.

Cut or blend the fried bread into crumbs, then stir into the lamb mixture to thicken the sauce.

Honeyed lamb

This rich, sweet Moroccan tagine was originally devised as a way of preserving meat before refrigeration. Make it 24 hours in advance, then reheat gently when required.
Serves 6

A pinch of saffron threads
1 tsp freshly ground
black pepper
1 tsp ground cinnamon
2 tsp ras el hanout (North
African herb and spice mix)
1kg (2lb) middle neck of lamb
with bone in
170g (6oz) raisins
3 onions, finely chopped
140g (5oz) blanched almonds
400g (14oz) honey
Juice of ½ lemon

Crush the saffron with the other spices and a pinch of salt using a pestle and mortar. Rub most of the mixture into the lamb and mix the remainder with the raisins.

Put the marinated lamb, onions, almonds and 170ml (6fl oz) water into a pan. Bring to a boil then cover and cook gently, stirring occasionally, for about 1 to 1¼ hours until the meat is almost tender – top up with more water if necessary to keep the meat from catching on the bottom of the pan.

Stir in the raisin mixture, honey and lemon juice and cook, uncovered, for 30 minutes until almost all the liquid has evaporated, leaving a rich, thick sauce. Serve with couscous.

Tray kibbeh

This Lebanese dish using minced lamb, bulghur and spices makes a delicious main course. It can also be served as an appetizer.

Serves 4–6

100ml (4fl oz) tomato juice
50ml (2fl oz) fresh
lemon juice
200g (7oz) bulghur
60g (2oz) wholewheat flour
450g (1lb) minced lamb
1 tsp paprika
½ tsp ground cumin
A large pinch of cayenne
1½ tbsp sesame seeds
60g (2oz) butter, melted
2 tbsp sunflower oil

For the filling:

1 tbsp olive oil
1 onion, finely chopped
12 oz minced lamb
60g (2oz) walnuts, chopped
½ tsp allspice

First make the kibbeh 'pastry'. Mix together the tomato juice, lemon juice, bulghur and 100ml (4fl oz) water. Leave to rest for 10 minutes.

Put 450g (1lb) minced lamb, the spices and the sesame seeds into a food processor and process until the meat is ground into a paste-like consistency. Gradually add the bulghur mixture, then season with salt and pepper. Tip into a bowl, mix well and chill for 2 hours.

Meanwhile, make the filling. Heat the olive oil in a large frying pan and fry the onion for 5 minutes until softened. Add the minced lamb and fry, stirring, for 5 to 10 minutes until the meat is browned. Drain off any excess fat, then stir in the nuts and allspice and season with salt and pepper.

Preheat the oven to 200°C (400°F/Gas mark 6).

Mix together the butter and sunflower oil and brush over the bottom of a square baking tin. Using wet hands, press half the pastry mixture into the base of the pan. Spoon over the filling, spreading it evenly. Press the remaining pastry over the top, pressing it up to the edges of the pan. Cut into eight slices and brush with the remaining sunflower mixture. Bake for 10 minutes, then lower the heat to 175°C (350°F/Gas mark 4) and bake for a further 30 minutes.

Let cool slightly, then lift out the slices and serve.

Spiced lamb topped with tomatoes

Cooked slowly under a blanket of well-browned onions, these lamb shanks become wonderfully succulent and tender.

Serves 6

Mix together the cinnamon, cumin, ginger, parsley and coriander. Divide the mixture and reserve half. Coat the lamb shanks in half the spice mixture, then chill for 3-4 hours.

Heat 2½ tbsp oil in a large heavy cooking pot. Add the onion, season with salt and cook gently, stirring occasionally, for 10 to 15 minutes until golden. Remove from the pan.

Preheat the oven to 160°C (325°F/Gas mark 3).

Add the marinated lamb to the pot, adding more oil if necessary, and cook for 10 to 15 minutes until browned all over. Season with salt and pepper, then add the remaining spice mixture and the cooked onions.

Put the tomato purée in a cup and blend in a little water. Add to the lamb with enough water almost to cover. Bring to the boil, cover with a tight-fitting lid then bake for 1 hour 40 minutes or until the lamb is cooked.

Add the tomatoes, cut-side down, to the pan, sprinkle with the sugar and return to the oven for 20 minutes or until everything is tender.

1½ tsp ground cinnamon
¼ tsp ground cumin
¼ tsp ginger
1 small bunch
parsley, chopped
1 small bunch
coriander, chopped
6 lamb shanks, each weighing
about 225g (½lb)
3 tbsp olive oil
1 large red onion, finely
chopped
1½ tbsp tomato purée
3 large, ripe tomatoes, peeled,
deseeded and halved
1–2 tsp white sugar

Sautéed lamb with aubergine

This quick, no-fuss recipe is a simple way to add fresh flavours to lamb cutlets.
Serves 4

3 tbsp olive oil
8 lamb cutlets, trimmed
2 large aubergines,
thickly sliced
2 garlic cloves, minced
6 large tomatoes, blanched,
skinned and thickly sliced
1 lemon, sliced, to garnish

For the sauce:

2 tbsp fresh mint, chopped,
plus extra to garnish
150ml (5fl oz) plain yogurt

Heat 1 tbsp olive oil in a wok over a high heat until almost smoking.
Add the lamb cutlets and fry for 5 minutes on each side until golden.
Remove from the wok and keep warm.

Add the remaining oil to the wok and fry the aubergine with the garlic
for 10 to 15 minutes until lightly browned on both sides. Add the
tomato slices and stir-fry for 1 minute. Season with salt and pepper,
then transfer to a serving dish. Top with the cutlets and garnish with
lemon slices and mint.

To make the sauce, mix together the mint and yogurt, season with black
pepper and serve with the lamb and vegetables.

Rack of lamb in a garlic crust

This is an easy recipe that makes an impressive roast to serve at the table.
Serves 4–6

Turn the lamb racks bone-side up and cut a narrow slit between each
cutlet at the meaty end. Slice 1 garlic clove and stuff each slit with a
sliver of the garlic and a blade of rosemary.

Put the lamb racks, fat side up, into an oiled roasting tin. Cut several
shallow slashes into the fat.

Mince the remaining garlic and mix with the breadcrumbs, jelly,
parsley and mustard. Season with salt and pepper, then smear over the
lamb racks. Leave to marinate for 1 to 2 hours.

Preheat the oven to 230°C (450°F/Gas mark 8) and roast the lamb for
25 to 35 minutes until browned and still a little pink in the centre.

2 racks of lamb, each
containing 4–6 cutlets, chined
3 garlic cloves
1 rosemary sprig
1 tbsp oil
3 tbsp fresh white
breadcrumbs
2 tbsp redcurrant
jelly, warmed
1 tbsp chopped parsley
½ tsp French mustard

Spicy lamb stew with mint and sage

Delicately tender lamb fillet is the perfect cut in this traditional Greek pilaf. Use twice the quantity of fresh mint and sage if you prefer.

Serves 6–8

50ml (2fl oz) olive oil
1kg (2lb) lean lamb fillet, cut into 2.5cm (1in) cubes
1 onion, chopped
2 carrots, diced
100ml (4fl oz) dry white wine
70g (2½ oz) slivered almonds
250g (9oz) long-grain rice
50g (2 oz) sultanas
½ tsp dried sage
1 tsp dried mint

Heat the oil in a large saucepan. Add the lamb and cook, turning regularly, until browned. Add the onion and carrots and cook for 5 minutes. Stir in the wine and season with salt and pepper. Bring to the boil, cover and cook for 10 minutes.

Meanwhile, toast the almonds in a heavy frying pan until lightly golden. Set aside.

Stir 1l (30fl oz) water into the meat mixture and simmer for 30 minutes, stirring occasionally. Add the rice, sultanas, sage and mint to the stew, then simmer, covered, for 30 to 35 minutes, adding a little extra water if necessary, until the rice is cooked and the meat is tender.

Lamb with apricot sauce

This delicious recipe is inspired by the classic Middle Eastern combination of lamb with apricots, a fusion given added sweetness here with the peanut butter-based sauce.

Serves 4

Cut the lamb into 2.5cm (1in) cubes and season. Thread onto skewers and grill, or cook in hot oil or melted butter in a frying pan until tender, approximately 5 minutes.

To prepare the sauce, melt the oil and butter together and add the garlic. Whisk in the puréed apricots and the peanut butter. Do not allow the peanut butter to become too hot; remove from the pan when half-melted. Add the lemon juice and season to taste. Serve with the lamb pieces. Garnish with parsley.

700g (1½ lb) lamb fillet
Salt and freshly ground
black pepper
Oil or butter, to fry
For the sauce:
50ml (2fl oz) vegetable oil
125g (4½ oz) butter
1 tsp garlic, minced
6 oz pitted apricots, puréed
50g (2oz) peanut butter
Juice of 1 lemon, to taste
Salt and freshly ground
black pepper
Parsley, to garnish

Lamb chops with cheese

An unusual but delicious combination of lamb and cheese, cooked in foil to retain all of the natural flavours.
Serves 4

2 tbsp butter
1 onion, sliced
2 garlic cloves, minced
4 lamb chump chops
3 tomatoes, sliced
3 tsp dried oregano
100g (4oz) Gruyère cheese,
thinly sliced

Preheat the oven to 175°C (350°F/Gas mark 4). Lay a large sheet of aluminium foil on a work surface.

Melt the butter in the frying pan and fry the onion and garlic for 3 minutes. Divide the onion mixture between the lamb chops together with the tomatoes, oregano and cheese. Season with salt and pepper.

Gather up the sides of the foil and pinch together to encase the chops. Transfer to a baking sheet and cook for 1½ to 2 hours until the meat is cooked through and tender.

Grilled butterflied leg of lamb

An easy, yet delicious, way to add stacks of flavour to a leg of lamb. Boning and butterflying the leg first will ensure it cooks quickly and evenly.

Serves 8–10

Put the lamb into a large dish. Put the garlic, chopped rosemary, sea salt, olive oil, lemon juice and black pepper in a bowl. Mix well, then rub into the lamb. Marinate for 4 hours or overnight in the refrigerator.

Preheat the barbecue or grill to high. Grill the lamb, covered (if your barbecue has a lid), for 30 to 40 minutes, turning regularly. Cook until just pink inside, then garnish with extra rosemary sprigs.

*3kg (6lb) leg of lamb, boned
and butterflied (ask your
butcher to do this or see
page 230)
8 garlic cloves, thinly sliced
4 tbsp chopped rosemary,
plus 3 sprigs
1 tbsp sea salt
50ml (2fl oz) olive oil
Juice of 2 lemons
2 tsp ground black pepper*

Tung-Po mutton

This dish is a great way of adding lots of flavour to mutton – the slow cooking time allows the meat to become meltingly tender.

Serves 4

Oil, for frying
450g (1lb) stewing mutton,
cut into 2cm (¾in) cubes
2 potatoes, cut into
2cm (¾in) cubes
2 carrots, cut into
2cm (¾in) cubes
2 tbsp soy sauce
1 tbsp sugar
2 scallions
1 slice ginger
1 garlic clove, crushed
1 tsp five-spice powder
3 tbsp rice wine or dry sherry
½ tsp Szechuan pepper

Heat the oil in a large frying pan or wok until almost smoking. Add the mutton and fry for 5 to 6 minutes until golden. Remove from the pan with a slotted spoon, then add the potatoes and carrots. Fry for 5 to 6 minutes until golden.

Put the mutton into a heavy cooking pot and cover with cold water. Add the remaining ingredients, except for the potato and carrot, then bring to the boil. Reduce the heat and simmer for 2 to 3 hours. Add the potato and carrot, cook for 5 minutes, then serve.

Lisbon liver

Thinly sliced liver that is marinated then cooked with prosciutto is traditionally associated with Lisbon, but is popular throughout Portugal.

Serves 4

Put the liver into a dish with the garlic, bay leaf, wine and vinegar. Season, then cover and chill for at least 4 hours or preferably overnight.

Remove the liver from the wine mixture – reserving the liquid – and pat dry with kitchen towels. Discard the bay leaf.

Heat the olive oil in a large pan. Add the prosciutto and cook until crisp. Add the marinated liver and cook for 3 minutes on each side. Transfer the meat to a warm plate, cover and keep warm.

Stir the reserved wine mixture into the pan and boil rapidly until reduced by about half. Pour over the liver and prosciutto and serve.

450g (1lb) lamb's liver,
thinly sliced
4 garlic cloves, minced
1 bay leaf
175ml (6fl oz) dry white wine
1 tbsp white wine vinegar
3 tbsp olive oil
50g (2oz) prosciutto or
bacon, chopped

CREDITS

The author would like to thank the following people and organisations for the information and advice they provided:

Trevor Amen, National Cattlemen's Beef Association (www.beefitswhatsfordinner.com)
American Lamb Board (www.americanlamb.com)
Nigel Armstrong (www.meatcity.ltd.uk)
National Pork Board (www.theotherwhitemeat.com)

BIBLIOGRAPHY

Chartered Institute of Environmental Health, *Food Safety First Principles* (Chadwick House Group, 2005)
Hugh Fearnley-Whittingstall, *The River Cottage Meat Book* (Hodder & Stoughton, 2004)
Aliza Green, *Field Guide to Meat* (Quirk Books, 2005)
Larousse Gastronomique (Hamlyn, 2001)
Harold McGee, *McGee on Food & Cooking* (Hodder & Stoughton, 2004)
John J. Mettler Jr, *Basic Butchering of Livestock and Game* (Storey Publishing, 2003)
Susan Spaull and Lucinda Bruce-Gardyne, *Leiths Techniques Bible* (Bloomsbury, 2003)
OXO Ltd, *The Book of Meat Cookery*
Charles Sinclair, *Dictionary of Food* (A & C Black, 2005)
Michael Van Straten, *Super Feast* (Little Books Ltd, 2005)